`D1331928`

CONTENTS

Page

HOLY
FIRE!

TRAVELS IN THE HOLY LAND

JILL DUDLEY

Published by
Orpington Publishers

Origination by
Creeds, Bridport, Dorset
01308 423411

*Cover design
and illustration by*
Clare E. Taylor

Printed and bound in the UK by
Berforts Information Press

ISBN 10: 0-9553834-5-5
ISBN 13: 978-0-9553834-5-8

PROLOGUE

My main aim for journeying through the Holy Land was to see the historic sites of the three major monotheistic religions: Judaism, Christianity and Islam. It was also for the ancient pagan gods, and those who came with Alexander the Great, and later with the Romans.

I also hoped that my wavering atheism would suddenly receive that blinding flash of enlightenment I have been waiting for all these years, leaving me with no doubt at all regarding the existence of God.

Harry is again my travelling companion. People tell me that Harry is the hero of my books and they should be called 'The Travels and Trials of Harry'. He is certainly my greatest support and sparring partner, and without him I suspect there'd be no book at all.

It is impossible to visit the country without immediately becoming conscious of the divisions there. I have all through the book tried to remain objective regarding the Jewish 'right to return' and the Palestinian 'right to remain'. If by the end, however, I explode an opinion and by that give offence to anyone, it is not intended; it is merely one opinion amongst the trillions in the vast ocean of them concerning that small strip of land once called Palestine and now Israel.

FROM LONDON TO JERUSALEM

CHAPTER

1

FLIGHT TO
THE HOLY LAND

"Christian pilgrimage or not, I don't believe in God," I said. "Well, not really – maybe just a little," I added.

Harry darted a look in all directions as though I'd shouted out my PIN number and all my money was at risk. He'd just told me that if we were asked to sing hymns or say prayers I was to toe the line to whatever was expected of us.

We were in the departure lounge at Heathrow, waiting for our El Al flight to Tel Aviv. My attention was drawn to the sound of chanting, and I saw a group of Jewish men standing before the plate-glass window, rocking backwards and forwards in prayer. They all had side curls hanging from under their black hats or skull-caps, and were dressed in long black coats, or black jackets with white threads hanging at the corners. The side curls were in obedience to God's command to the Levites not to '...round off the hair on your temples.' (Leviticus 19:27).

In truth, I rather envied those who had faith, and was more than happy to fly with them under the protective umbrella of their God. For me it was as reassuring as seeing a black cat cross my path, or glimpsing the new moon in the sky and not through glass.

It was amazing that Harry had agreed to this trip. It seemed as though some unseen hand had planted in my mind a strong desire to see Jerusalem, and this same unseen hand had miraculously erased from Harry's mind all objections. His only stipulation had been that we travel with a reputable company and in a group.

"There's a Canon taking us. We can't go wrong with a Canon in charge," I'd told Harry when I'd found an organized tour whose itinerary included all the places I particularly wanted to see.

"Hum. We'll be safe with a Canon, I suppose," was Harry's comment. Another protective umbrella.

The Canon in question was seated opposite and I eyed him tentatively, examining the long slightly morose face, thinning grey hair and hangdog expression. He had, in fact, a kindly look, unlike his well-built wife who appeared fierce but whose features softened into a sweet smile when spoken to.

Terrorism in Israel at the time had been causing many would-be travellers to Israel to stay away. But, as I told Harry, the media always zoomed in on the worst atrocities, and no Canon would venture to the Holy Land leading his flock if the Foreign Office advised against it.

While we waited in the departure lounge, I tried to make eye contact with the Orthodox Jews – the men had now returned to their families. Surely I could catch the eye of one of them and smile? But no, they were totally preoccupied with themselves. It was as if we Christian travellers didn't exist for them.

★

We have taken off and are on our way. I am surprised and pleased to find myself seated next to one of the Jewish families with Harry on my other side beside the window. I note that there are no Arabs to be seen on this flight. The young mother on my right is cradling a baby, and has two other small children across the aisle from her. Her pale-faced husband is seated beside them, his side-curls dangling in front of his ears, a skull-cap on his head. I've heard that Orthodox Jews refuse to get into conversation with those not of their faith, but I can't resist chancing my luck. I ask the attractive young mother beside me if she minds me asking a question.

"Of course not!" she replies at once. She retrieves a baby's bottle from a bag at her feet, then tosses back her straight dark hair which has fallen over her handsome, smiling face. "Ask as many questions as you like," she invites.

I want to know why some of the young Jewish women have their heads covered with what look like floppy bath caps. She replies at once that it is to hide their hair.

"So why don't you hide your hair?" I ask.

"Oh, but I do. I wear a wig," she answers.

"A wig? Really?" I'm full of admiration, and recall the ill-fitting wigs I've seen on some elderly Jewish women. "Your wig is really most attractive!" I say. "What's the reason for it?" I enquire.

"It's expected as soon as you marry," she answers. "It's to stop you being sexually attractive to other men."

"Ah." I don't see the logic in this as I actually think she's very attractive in her wig.

"Do you ever take it off?" I ask.

"Never," she answers.

"Never? Not even at home?"

"No."

Maybe she hasn't heard me correctly, but I don't like to probe too deeply. She goes on to tell me how in Jerusalem there is a booming business in wig-making for newly-weds, and I think how I would like a wig so I need never bother with my hair.

She rearranges the baby on her arm and feeds it with the bottle. I notice that her husband, who has taken off his black jacket, looks skinny and unattractive in his white shirt; but he is very active in keeping his two older children occupied during the course of the journey.

I now ask her why the men have white threads hanging from their black jackets, something I've never seen before. Ah, she says, those are called 'Tzitzit' and represent the six hundred and thirteen commandments. I remember reading the many verses in Exodus in which God commands in detail how his Israelites are to conduct their daily lives. So lengthy are the commands that I skimmed through them without taking them in. Six hundred and thirteen!

But I really like this young woman seated beside me. She is extraordinarily efficient at managing her children and appears very happy to talk.

"Why are there so many Orthodox families on the plane?" I enquire.

"We're all returning from spending Passover with our families in England," she replies. She caresses her small daughter who is standing by her knee, her head lowered to her lap. "We have to travel today because tomorrow the term starts."

I glance at her young family and suppose that she must be referring to her husband. Certain Orthodox Jews, I know, spend their lives studying Jewish scripture and the law. Fundamental Jews have considerable political clout and are great believers in the coming of the Messiah at the End of Time. I've read that in Israel there is respect for them because it's thought that it is through their scrutiny of the laws and total obedience to God's commandments (all six hundred and thirteen of them) that the security and welfare of Israel depends.

"Are you Haredim?" I find myself asking. I'm not too sure if I have the word right but have conjured it up out of the dim recesses of memory, having recently read a book on Jewish fundamentalism.

"Yes," comes the reply, and she bends down to the open bag at her feet and pulls out a hand towel to wipe dribble away from the baby's chin.

I know that Haredi Jews are ultra-Orthodox. The word Haredi comes from the Hebrew word for 'fear' *(harada)*, one who fears God. They live in isolated communities and their lives centre around the study of Torah, prayer and family.

So here I am travelling with them. Such a charming family, I think.

There is a change about of the children and the father takes the baby. I now have the three year old son seated beside me with paper and crayons. He has large brown eyes, wears a skull-cap and, instead of side curls, has long wisps of baby side hair. I smile down at him and get a squirm and an impish smile back. He grows tired of drawing something with his yellow crayon, so I turn on the video in front of the seat and try to interest him in a cartoon. The mother, who is now across the aisle, leans over and says: "Do you mind, we don't allow them to watch television." I turn it off. Soon she is back in the seat beside me, no doubt so that I can't contaminate her young son with heathenish modern ideas. I notice that her husband now has the baby on one arm, and is quietly rocking backwards and forwards over his Torah which is in his other hand. Why, I ask his wife, does he rock like that?

"Because some passages are very difficult to understand and it helps him to concentrate," comes the answer. After a while I notice that the restless baby is asleep on the father's arm, and in no time the father himself is asleep over his Torah. Interesting. Maybe he's been studying the six hundred and thirteen commandments.

In time I learn from the young mother that hers was an arranged marriage. Her father is a Rabbi in London and her husband's father is principal of a Jewish school there. I'm far too polite to enquire about her feelings regarding this. Her three children aged three and under reveal there's a new generation of ultra-Orthodox Jews growing up to defend their country with their prayers, their scripture studies and what they believe to be Yahweh's decrees and purpose for them. They are those descendants of Abraham multiplied 'as the stars of heaven'. (Exodus 32:13).

I feel the need to stretch my legs, so I get up and walk around the aisles for a while, noting the many sleeping passengers. I catch the eye of the Canon's wife seated beside her drowsing husband, and she gives me her surprisingly sweet smile. Soon I am again among the Orthodox Jews. A tall young man in a skull-cap stands in the aisle with a bundle in his arms wrapped in a shawl. I break all convention and smile at him, and ask what's in the bundle – a silly question. I'm surprised he doesn't rebuff me and turn on his heel but, instead, he lowers his bundle for inspection and I see the minute sleeping face of a newborn baby.

"Three weeks old," he says proudly.

"Three weeks?"

"He was born in New York," he remarks.

"Really?" I'm even more surprised. To have been born in New York and to have already travelled to London for Passover, and now to be on the way to the land of his ancestors is no mean feat for a three week old baby.

I return to my seat.

Half an hour before we are due to land, many of the Orthodox men gather before the exit and once more, with a great display of rocking from the waist, chant prayers. Yet again I find it curiously reassuring.

That first morning we sat up in bed with mugs of tea. I opened my notebook and wrote: *Well, we're here in Jerusalem! Most exciting after all the planning, and the usual anxieties of missing the train, the bus, the flight – a hundred possible obstacles to making the trip.*

I'll start with our arrival at Tel Aviv airport. It must be significant that there were no airport notices written in Arabic; they were all either in Hebrew or English. The lack of military presence was also surprising – nothing visible at the airport, none on the road to Jerusalem, no armoured cars or soldiers to be seen anywhere. There wasn't any security screening either when we entered our hotel – all very odd and not at all what I expected. In Egypt we'd had to pass through strict security checks before entering our hotels. Any terrorist could come in here and plant a bomb if he wanted to.

Odd to think that this time yesterday we were still at home! Flitting around the world is really dead easy!

I closed my notebook, got out of bed and went over to the window. It looked out onto a concrete building opposite. The hotel delivery yard was two storeys below with a van driving into it, and a lorry backing into position to unload crates of bottles. A sparrow twittered on the neighbouring window ledge before flying to the next. Looking up I could see a triangle of sky, but it appeared colourless and didn't reveal if the day was overcast or if it was merely the early morning light.

"So what's on the agenda today?" Harry asked from his bed.

I found the printed sheet of paper outlining the day's itinerary and looked at it. "The Mount of Olives and the Garden of Gethsemane," I said.

"What exactly happened there, I forget?" Harry opened our bag of medication and examined the contents – Paracetamol for headaches, Imodium for upset stomachs, laxative for the opposite, sleeping pills for insomnia, nasal congestion pills, cough lozenges, rescue remedy for shock, antiseptic cream for cuts, anti-mosquito ointment, etc., etc. We were complete hypochondriacs when travelling, alarmed by the slightest ache or pain for fear it might get worse.

Stories of Jesus and his disciples and parables and miracles floated unanchored around in my mind. I had to admit I couldn't remember exactly what or why or where many things had happened.

"Not to worry," said Harry easily, "we'll no doubt find out soon enough."

"And we finish the day with the Yad Vashem Holocaust Memorial," I added, having skimmed through the afternoon agenda.

"That'll be interesting." Harry was more into modern history and politics than religion which was a mere embellishment to life – well, a sort of balm to mental stress. He opened his mouth wide and placed a pill on the back of his tongue before gulping it down with water. I noticed it was a Paracetemol.

"Do you have a headache?" I asked.

"Only the tiniest," he answered. "Just a precaution."

I am sitting under a fig tree and enjoying a bit of peace while the others are being shown the garden by a rather tiresome American woman. I think I'm in the doghouse with Harry because I'm not trailing around with everyone. But the woman said we could rest if we liked, and so I'm resting – well, writing up my notes.

I want to jot down what we've done so far today before it goes out of my head. We are in what I think is a Christian Zionist centre. Christian Zionists want to hurry on the 'second coming' and the end of the world, or something of the sort.

When we first arrived here we were shown into a semi-darkened room and sat around a long low table on which were numerous small bowls of kosher food, the sort Jesus as a Jew would have eaten, we were told. We were all about to help ourselves when this elderly American woman with cropped hair and a blue rinse entered busily. She greeted us, and then began to hold forth at great length about the food we were hoping to eat. After about fifteen minutes she eventually said: "And now enjoy what the good Lord has provided." I'd just managed to swallow a morsel of unleavened bread, when she began all over again, and we had to endure another ten minute monologue about things expected and unexpected. She's really got religion in a big way. She's why I'm sitting here and not trailing around listening to her irritating American voice twanging on about the joys of Christian faith and the hope of life everlasting. Her eyes have that other-worldly glow about them which comes with fanatical belief. She talks slowly and with emphasis, pausing every now and then to smile reassuringly at us.

This morning we were fairly whizzed around churches on the Mount of Olives. Because of the Gospels there was a certain holiness to the stony terrain with its silver-leafed olive trees and tall, dark green cypresses. The early morning haze was gone and there was a deep blue sky – quite warm (now hot) but with a cooling breeze. The churches were all twentieth century built on earlier foundations and run by the Franciscans. The Roman Catholics seem to have the monopoly of these churches. It was quite helpful having the relevant bits of the Gospels read aloud at the various places we visited.

We have a Palestinian Christian tour guide called Michael, a stocky middle-aged fellow with an olive complexion, small clipped moustache, quite sexy brown eyes, and thick greying hair which looks as though he's just run his fingers through it. Occasionally he says something and his face lights up with a mischievous smile.

Making herself fairly conspicuous among us is an Irish girl who seems to be travelling alone. She's about thirty, has a mop of dark curly hair, a baked potato shaped head, small grey eyes and a retroussé nose which she holds up to the window of the coach like a dog sniffing the air. She's very inquisitive and keeps asking questions in a singsong Irish brogue, such as: "Can you see Golgotha from here?" or "So who's the architect, then?" I suspect that Michael's becoming wary of her as she keeps up with him as he leads the way – clip-clopping alongside in uncomfortable looking wedged sandals and asking numerous questions. Sometimes she marches away from us all clutching her shoulder-bag under her arm, hair flouncing around her face and looking purposeful, before homing back on us. There seems to be no reason for this, and I've seen her do it several times now.

We appear to be two groups who have combined, one led by a well built Scottish minister, an ex-soldier, stand-no-nonsense sort of man, and us English lot led by the Canon. Because of the political uncertainties out here neither group managed to get the numbers required to make up a viable party, so they have amalgamated.

There's another amusing character, a white-haired woman (must be over seventy) who's the leader of a bunch of W.I. women. She strides around with her new digital camera making comments. She's full of good humour and likes to think she's broad minded, though in fact has decided views. For instance, at breakfast this morning she told me she's a prominent member of her church and attends regularly for the good of the community as part of discipline and faith. Faith, she says, is not belief but commitment and trust which seems to me to be a denial of reason, but she's so likeable that it is obviously good for her and others, I suppose. Come to think of it, faith and trust are fine, it's blind belief that is suspect.

We were taken first to the 12th century Crusader Chapel of the Ascension on the summit of the Mount of Olives where Jesus is said to have been lifted up to heaven forty days after his Resurrection. Forty seems to be a mystical number – forty years wandering in the wilderness by the Israelites; forty days when Jesus was tempted by Satan; forty days before ascending to heaven –

Inside the Chapel of the Ascension we were shown what is claimed to be the footprint in the rock left by Jesus when he was taken up. I thought it remarkably large for a man's print, and not much like a foot – a Holy Ghost of a one perhaps.

Nearby was the 17th century Mosque of the Ascension which I'd have liked to have gone to. It was built there because they too believe in Jesus' ascension, not as the Son of God, but as God's prophet.

Most memorable this morning was the Church of Dominus Flevit, which Michael told us means 'tear drop'. The building is designed to represent an inverted tear drop because it was where Jesus looked out towards Jerusalem and wept because he foresaw the destruction of the city. Its western window was an impressively simple arched one with clear glass and a wrought-iron design of thorns with a central chalice silhouetted against the sky. At eye level below these wrought iron silhouettes was a fantastic view of old Jerusalem with the gold Dome of the Rock rising up above the buildings.

Further down a walled alleyway we came to the Garden of Gethsemane and the Church of the Agony. It was there that Jesus had despaired of his disciples who'd fallen asleep instead of watching and praying as he'd asked them to: 'Could you not watch?'.

Outside the church were some ancient olive trees with gnarled trunks and massive girths which may well have existed at the time of Christ, Michael said. He also pointed out a thorn bush to us, with its thorns about an inch long spaced along the stem every six inches or so. The crown placed on the head of Jesus at his crucifixion was made from a thorn bush.

From there we were taken down to a lookout point where we had another panoramic view of Jerusalem, to its old city and ancient walls, and the Dome of the Rock rising gleaming gold above the huddled buildings like the glint of the rising sun. Michael pointed out the other places of note: the grey dome of the Al Aqsa Mosque which apparently is the next most holiest mosque after Mecca and Medina; the smaller Dome of the Spirit, and beyond these the wider grey dome of the Church of the Holy Sepulchre.

Below us was the Kidron Valley and the Jewish cemetery in a large barren area filled with numerous higgledy-piggledy white tombs, like strewn children's building blocks. The tombs are aligned to the east towards the rising sun which, of course, is a symbol of resurrection. I wonder whether the Jews originally got the idea from their forebears the Israelites when they were slaves in Egypt? There the east bank of the Nile was thought to represent the daily resurrection of the sun and the renewal of life. It is, in fact, a cult statue of a pagan god idea too, as each temple's cult statue is placed to face the east and the rising sun.

Michael told us that the cemetery was located east of the city walls because the Jews believed that at the coming of the Messiah he would reveal himself on the Mount of Olives as prophesied by Zechariah. When he comes, he is expected to make a triumphal entry into Jerusalem to the sounding of the shofar accompanied by Elijah. When Michael said that, the Irish girl at once blurted out that the Messiah had already come with Jesus, whereupon Michael explained that that was the Christian belief but the Jews were still waiting for him.

Oh, yes, before I forget! I must write down how the W.I. woman, just before we got onto the coach at the lookout point, suddenly called out: "Come on, girls! this is where we sing 'Jerusalem'!" In no time they all burst into song much to Michael's surprise and our amusement. While they were holding forth the W.I. woman, who was herself singing, hurried around the group with her camera to take a shot of them all in full voice. Afterwards I found myself beside her as we were waiting to get on the coach and couldn't resist telling her that I actually found the words totally peculiar. I mean, did we really want to build Jerusalem in England's green and pleasant land? She was very good humoured about it. She was the sort of woman I could say such things to because she was so cheerful and amiable. "By golly! I've never been asked that before! You may well ask!" Harry tried to prod me onto the coach fast but not before the W.I. woman (who was quite unruffled) explained that it was a thundering good tune and when they all sang it in the Albert Hall to the crescendoing of the organ it was an unforgettable experience. Besides, she said, William Blake was *one of our greatest English poets and a mystic, and tradition was tradition – difficult to change. I noticed she gave Harry a could-control-your-wife-better sort of look which, I'm glad to say, I don't think he noticed.*

I think I can hear them now crunching back along the gravel path. I can hear the American woman's voice holding forth still – probably pointing to every weed and flower Jesus would have trampled on or seen – Have to stop. Here they come! We go on to the Yad Vashem Holocaust Memorial next.

Located on Mount Herzl, seven kilometres west of the city of Jerusalem, the Yad Vashem Holocaust Memorial occupied a vast landscaped area and had a surprising aura of peace and tranquillity about it. Mount Herzl was named after the great nineteenth century Zionist, Theodor Herzl (1860-1904) whose life work was to swing the opinion of all who had influence and political clout in favour of allowing Jews to return to their 'homeland'. He died over thirty years before the horror of the holocaust.

The etymology of the word 'holocaust' comes from the Greek meaning 'a complete burning' or 'whole burnt sacrifice'. The anti-Semitic period under the Nazi regime, and the humiliation and would-be extermination of the Jews (Hitler's 'final solution') sent shock waves throughout the world which added weight to the 'return' idea. Many trees on this carefully landscaped area, we were told, were dedicated to those heroic individuals who risked their lives to save Jews at that time.

We were taken first to the Hall of Remembrance, a sober building with walls of interlocking basalt boulders. A pebble mosaic floor had on it the names of twenty-one concentration camps. Centrally placed was the Eternal

Flame rising from a bronze container shaped like a broken goblet, and before it a crypt containing the ashes of Holocaust victims brought from the extermination camps. Today civic and international dignitaries come to lay wreaths, each one, no doubt, with the thought and prayer that men must never be allowed to oppress, suppress or attempt an extermination of a people ever again – never, never!

We were then led to the Children's Memorial Hall, a vast domed building, the interior of which was in semi-darkness. We had to keep to a wooden walkway, holding on to a rail while feeling our way around. In the dome were illuminated five giant photographs of young children, and around them were bright stars in the dark heavens representing the one and a half million children who had perished at the hands of the Nazis. Every thirty seconds or so a voice proclaimed the name of a child-victim and his or her nationality. I was struck by the fact there were no British sounding names.

We were given an hour to wander at leisure during which time I recalled Menachem Begin whose autobiography *The Revolt* I had recently read. He was a Russian Jew born in Eastern Europe in 1913, and his writing was brilliantly vivid and articulate. He described his own persecution in prison as a young man, his Zionist aspirations, and his arrival in Palestine during World War II. As a pioneer Zionist he rebelled against the British Mandate, and joined the Irgun/Stern Gang. I couldn't help but admire Begin's sheer audacity, his courage when facing perilous situations, and his ability to endure unbelievable hardship.

Begin had vision, and acted on his own initiative. There seemed to be a driving force within him. Such people are so convinced they are in the right, that the rights of others fade into insignificance although they pay lip service to them in public. Menachem Begin became a political figure, and made promises he was unable to keep. He announced in his radio broadcast in May, 1948, when the new independent State of Israel was declared: '...justice must be the supreme ruler, the ruler over all rulers. There must be no tyranny. The Ministers and officials must be the servants of the nation and not their masters. There must be no exploitation. There must be no man within our country – be he citizen or foreigner – compelled to go hungry, to want for a roof over his head, or to lack elementary education... Righteousness must be the guiding principle in our relations amongst ourselves...'

So many good intentions! This astonishingly ruthless man, a survivor and obdurate Zionist fighter; a man who masterminded numerous terrorist attacks against the British, the most notorious of them being the blowing up in 1946 of the British military administration centre in the King David Hotel in which ninety-one people were killed; who brushed aside as lying Arab propaganda the Israeli massacre and destruction of the Arab village of Deir Yassin in 1948; who then used it ruthlessly to terrorize other Palestinian villages to prompt inhabitants to flee; never wavered for a moment from belief in his own (and, therefore, Israel's) 'righteousness'. He wrote in his book: 'Impracticable faith? Maybe. Yet faith is perhaps stronger than reality; faith itself creates reality.'

Once the State of Israel had been established in 1948, this much-to-be-admired, and also much-to-be-feared, man went on to work tirelessly for peace – so long as Israel remained in control. For this he was awarded the Nobel Peace Prize in 1978, an award which to many might seem at odds with the word 'Peace'.

As we wandered along a path to return to our coach, we met the Canon and his wife approaching hand in hand from another pathway. The Canon's wife gave me a sorrowful smile. "Very harrowing," she remarked. She was slightly breathless and clearly suffered from the heat which gave her a high colour and accentuated her blue eyes.

"Almost unbelievable Man's inhumanity to Man," the Canon remarked as we walked along the path together.

I wanted to ask him why he thought these calamities came about, and why, if God existed, he had withheld himself and allowed his 'chosen' to suffer such atrocities. Of course if God didn't exist that would explain it, I wanted to say. But instead I talked about the attractive landscaping of the place, and all was peace and harmony as we wandered back to the coach.

On the drive back to our hotel, Michael informed us that the following day was Israel's Memorial Day when they would remember their dead, and the day following they would be celebrating their Day of Independence. The streets everywhere were festooned with Israeli flags; they flew from office blocks and hung from apartment windows. Even cars speeding along the roads had small Star of David flags fluttering from their car windows like football supporters before the World Cup.

There was no doubt who were the masters here now in Israel.

Before I switched off the light that night I opened my notebook and wrote:

So what do I think of Jerusalem after one day? Well... a cauldron of conflicting ingredients with the lid on it. A little more heat and it'll boil over requiring a lot of cleaning up.

Religion's very odd!

Before I forget! Since Michael told us about Jewish expectation of the fulfilment of prophecy regarding their Messiah, it's occurred to me that Jesus, being a Jew and believing he was the Messiah, would have acted out the role according to prophetic pronouncements OR, come to that, Matthew, Mark, Luke, etc. would or could have written the Messiah expectations/fulfilment of prophecies into the Gospels. It's an idea worth pondering over.

Harry's now snoring which is good as it shows he's asleep and not in need of a sleeping pill. Tomorrow we visit Bethlehem. Exciting. I'm really looking forward to it.

THE CHURCH OF THE NATIVITY

CHAPTER

2

BETHLEHEM

"Just hold your passports up so the Israeli soldier who comes on board can see," said the Canon.

"This will be interesting!" said the W.I. woman seated behind me. "I suppose I'm not allowed to take a photograph?"

"Please don't!" came the decisive warning from the Canon's wife.

From where I sat on the coach I could see the Canon's long face becoming even more morose and watchful as we approached the check-point at the West Bank. A metal hurdle blocked the road together with a line of concrete blocks. I noticed a group of Palestinians seated listlessly under a tree. They must have been refused permission to pass through.

This was our first experience of an Israeli check-point. I had a multitude of subversive thoughts, things I would have liked to have said aloud, but I remained silent.

An armed Israeli soldier passed down between us checking our passports, before descending from the coach looking sheepish. I inwardly raged at this gun authority and our lack of courage to say a word because it would cause trouble and an inevitable and inconvenient delay to this our trip to Bethlehem.

"Well, we got through that easily enough," said the W.I. woman brightly, and her companions laughed. "Wouldn't want to be faced with that gun, by golly! But suppose they can't be too careful."

The driver started up the coach and we drove on, manoeuvring around the road-block.

For a while we followed alongside the newly-built, toweringly massive Israeli security wall with its round watch-towers − built to defend themselves against Palestinian terrorism was the Israeli explanation for it. The ugly construction went on relentlessly, separating Israeli land from Palestinian, and only too often cutting through Palestinian olive groves and orchards, so that an unfortunate farmer found himself unable to pass easily from one part of his smallholding to another, or to move his livestock to their water.

But we were on a Christian pilgrimage from Britain and had no need to concern ourselves with these inconveniences and frustrations experienced by the Palestinians.

Soon we were driving through Bethlehem with its crowded streets of featureless white houses, and were put down in Manger Square.

We gathered at the entrance to the Church of the Nativity where Michael was waiting for us. He began to speak about early Christianity, about the Persian conquest in 614 A.D., the coming of the Moslems a few decades later, and the subsequent Crusaders. He then turned towards the Canon who was waiting to read a passage from Isaiah 11:1-5.

"'There shall come forth a shoot from the stump of

Jesse, and a branch shall grow out of his roots. And the Spirit of the Lord shall rest upon him, the spirit of wisdom and understanding, the spirit of counsel and might, the spirit of knowledge and the fear of the Lord. And his delight shall be in the fear of the Lord. He shall not judge by what his eyes see, or decide by what his ears hear; but with righteousness he shall judge the poor, and decide with equity for the meek of the earth; and he shall smite the earth with the rod of his mouth, and with the breath of his lips he shall slay the wicked. Righteousness shall be the girdle of his waist, and faithfulness the girdle of his loins.'" He closed his Bible, murmuring: "The root of Jesse – " and many in our group nodded appreciatively.

Michael took over from the Canon and pointed to an arched outline on the exterior wall which had been the original and much larger entrance to the church. It had been blocked up and reduced to its present diminutive doorway for defence purposes, he said.

So here we were at the Church of the Nativity. The church had been founded by Constantine in the early fourth century. His mother, Helena, travelling in the Holy Land in the fourth century, had had a good nose for sniffing out important sites in the life of Jesus. To find out the location of Christ's birth Helena had turned to the Gospels, though only Luke and Matthew had the story of the Nativity in them and, rather strangely, these two books were not written until at least forty years after the death of Christ – the earliest (St. Mark's) being dated around 70 A.D.

Surprisingly too the Gospels had, in fact, been written several decades later than the epistles of St. Paul which were penned around 50 A.D. – I say surprisingly because the Gospels in the New Testament are placed before the letters of St. Paul. St. Paul never spoke or wrote about Christ's birth and life but concentrated on how Christians should conduct their lives. It was Paul who established the thinking and disciplines of the new Christian religion. In contrast, the Gospel writers, following on from St. Paul, elaborated on the life of Jesus, on his miracles and his teachings. Until the Gospels, the life of Christ had been spread by word of mouth, not through any written records.

I was astonished to discover that by the second century A.D., far from being remembered as the birthplace of Jesus and, therefore, the advent of Christianity, Bethlehem had had a sacred grove dedicated to Adonis beloved of Aphrodite, goddess of love. Equally astonishing is the Semitic name Adonis which means 'the Lord', and this 'Lord' met an early death and was resurrected every year in the spring.

This resurrection of Adonis (the 'Lord') had been celebrated annually long before the birth of Christ. His worshippers would sow symbolic seeds which grew rapidly and as quickly withered, and they followed in procession with these so-called 'gardens of Adonis' together with an effigy of his dead body. He was widely known in the East by the name Tammuz and was mentioned in the Old Testament by the prophet Ezekiel who commented on the women of Jerusalem weeping for Tammuz at the north gate of Solomon's temple. (Ezekiel 8:14).

In this way the 'Passion' of Adonis was very similar to the Passion of Christ and, with the establishment of Christianity, many converts continued sowing plates of seed and for a long time combined their old custom with the Christian Good Friday procession, following the effigy of the dead body not of Adonis but of Christ.

We entered the Church of the Nativity. Inside there

was an immense feeling of space and mystery. It was run by the Greek Orthodox Church whose purpose always was to emphasize the spiritual by working on the five senses – sight, hearing, smell, taste and touch. Inside the church tall marble columns soared upwards, topped by their magnificent Corinthian capitals. The eye, however, was drawn forward, past the columns, past the ornately patterned gold and wine-red pulpit, past the equally spectacular bishop's throne, to the magnificent *iconostasis* (the sanctuary screen) of wrought silver with its three tiers of icons. Suspended from the roof were numerous gleaming icon lamps, and a central hanging ornate brass chandelier dripping with crystal drops.

"This is where they barricaded themselves in," said the Irish girl coming up beside me.

"Who?" I asked.

"Those Palestinians – April, 2002," she said.

I had quite forgotten the incident, and remembered only vaguely that there had been something on T.V. about it. The word 'incident' is a bad one – incident it might have been to us in Britain who were kept informed about it whilst it was ongoing, but an unforgettable endurance and agony to all those who were caught up in it.

"There were two hundred of them barricaded in here," said the Irish girl.

"I forget why it happened?" I asked, ashamed of my forgetfulness which displayed a degree of indifference to the calamity of others.

"Oh, it was the usual," she replied dismissively. "Israeli reprisals because there was a Palestinian attack on them in some village nearby."

"You mean the Israelis attacked Bethlehem for that?"

"Oh, yes. They sent in tanks in the early morning and

bombarded the houses."

"That's quite despicable!"

"They have to defend their own people," she replied decisively. She turned her attention back to the church. "This is beautiful," she remarked. "I like this!" And she went off to take a closer look at some of the original floor mosaics displayed under glass depicting fruit and geometric patterns.

The Emperor Justinian had rebuilt the basilica (in the form it was now) in the sixth century and, apparently, on the facade of the church where we had entered, there had been a mosaic of the Magi (sometimes referred to as the three wise men, or three kings) worshipping the baby Jesus in the manger. It is believed that when the Persians invaded in 614 A.D. they destroyed many Christian churches but spared this one because they'd recognized the priestly robes as being those of their Persian Magi, the priests of Ahura Mazda, the Persian deity, whom Zarathustra (the famous Persian prophet who lived many centuries B.C.), proclaimed as the one and only true God.

When Islam had swept up from Arabia in the seventh century they, unlike the Persians, had respected all Christian churches because in the Koran Jesus was regarded as a Prophet of Allah. In fact the Caliph Umar himself had used a corner of the Church of the Nativity for his prayers.

Harry came up and told me that the others were going down into the crypt to see the cave where Jesus was believed to have been born.

"Please! mind your step as you go down!" Michael called as we queued up and then bent double to go through the low doorway and down steep steps leading to the crypt. "And mind your heads!" he warned.

As I descended I could hear voices from below

singing *Away in a Manger*. It's quite odd how carols stamp themselves on the mind creating a vision of a two thousand year old story. When we got down to the crypt we found a group dressed in surplices standing before a small chapel and singing and swaying in a happy clappy manner. We were told they were Armenians who came daily at noon.

Soon we ourselves were following the Scottish minister's lead and singing *While Shepherds Watched Their Flocks by Night*. Michael, our guide, had earlier made the point that it was highly unlikely that sheep would have been out in December as there would have been snow and the sheep would have been brought in by then. Jesus was more likely to have been born in September, he thought. I was surprised he'd been prepared to throw out a controversial point in front of the Canon, but no one seemed concerned.

In fact, I'd read that the early Church had conveniently used the pagan calendar for important events in its liturgical year, Christmas being one of them. As it was quite unknown what date Jesus had been born, it was decided (and not until the fourth century) to celebrate his birth at the time of the winter solstice when there was a Roman festival 'Sol Invictus' which celebrated the increasing light of the sun. I found that fascinating because Jesus, the Gospels said, called himself the 'Light of the world'. In pagan times also there had been a 'light of the world'. Apollo had had the epithet 'Phoebos' – Phoebos Apollo – Phoebos, the shining one, the light of the world. He had at one time been equated with the sun.

J.G. Frazer in *The Golden Bough* wrote about the nativity of Jesus and the early Church adopting pagan nativity stories. He wrote: 'The ritual of the nativity, as it appears to have been celebrated in Syria and Egypt, was remarkable. The celebrants retired into certain inner shrines, from which at midnight they issued with a loud cry, "The Virgin has brought forth! The light is waxing!" The Egyptians even represented the new-born sun by the image of an infant which on his birthday, the winter solstice, they brought forth and exhibited to his worshippers. No doubt the Virgin who thus conceived and bore a son on the twenty-fifth of December was the great Oriental goddess whom the Semites called the Heavenly Virgin or simply the Heavenly Goddess; in Semitic lands she was a form of Astarte.'

The Greeks, of course, identified Astarte with Aphrodite who adored Adonis (the Lord). Fascinating!

I found myself peering into St. Jerome's Cave. St. Jerome had settled in Bethlehem in 386 A.D. He was renowned for his translation of the Bible from Greek into Latin. St. Jerome had been adamant about the perpetual virginity of the Virgin Mary, insisting on it being an undeniable and miraculous truth. So much in Christianity required people not to question, not to investigate or probe too deeply.

It is curious that at the time of Jesus himself nothing at all had been recorded regarding his birth. Seventy years is really quite a long time to keep quiet about a spectacular event. The writers of the time merely touched on the fact that Christians were emerging; they never elaborated on anything concerning the life or death or Resurrection of Jesus. And, apparently, there was no Roman record of his trial and crucifixion, even though the Romans, I understood, had been meticulous about keeping written accounts of their judicial proceedings.

Near to St. Jerome's cave was Joseph's cave where tradition has it an angel came to Joseph in a dream telling him to flee with Mary and the baby to Egypt. This was to escape the wrath of King Herod who wanted to massacre all boy babies for fear that one of them might be the future king of the Jews. According to Michael male baby bones had been found down there.

But why, I wondered, would Herod, who had plenty of sons and, therefore, heirs to the throne, be remotely interested in a new-born baby descended from the House of David? And, in fact, so alarmed by the thought that he ordered the massacre of all baby boys at that time? Some believe it was a recycling of the story from the Old Testament of the birth of Moses when the Pharaoh of the day had issued an edict that all male Israelite boys were to be killed.

The Scottish Minister came to rout me out. Had I seen the star, he enquired? The star? Oh, THE star!

He led me back to where *Away in a Manger* had been sung, and drew back a small curtain which partly concealed the small silver star embedded in marble in a cavity in the rock (presumably the manger?). All photographs I'd seen of it made it appear considerably larger than it actually was.

"It's easy to overlook," said the Minister. "Makes you realize that the Lord Jesus was a wee bairn."

I wondered whether there was any connection between the Star of David, the star followed by the wise men, and the planet Venus which represented the goddess of love. To continue with James Frazer's *The Golden Bough*, in it he described how at Antioch the rites of Adonis began with the appearance of Venus as the morning star. There was great excitement among the people when this symbolic goddess of love was sighted, as though the goddess herself was coming to bring her lover back to life. According to Frazer too the Emperor Julian the Apostate arrived at Antioch when the morning star was first visible and the people, whom he believed were greeting him, shouted that the Star of Salvation had dawned upon them in the East. This, so Frazer suggested, might well have been the same star which had guided the wise men (Persian Magi) to Bethlehem.

"You know," I said to Harry, "that Hellenistic ideas were imposed on the Jews as a result of Alexander the Great's conquests? They were imposed by the Seleucids who were hated by the Jews, especially when they set up an altar to Zeus in the temple in Jerusalem – and sacrificed swine on it. Anyway, this was a hundred and something years before Christ. The interesting thing being that the Jews at the time, under their freedom fighters who were called Maccabees, managed to beat off these Seleucids and restore Jewish worship in the temple. And – AND, mind you! – it happened on the day of the winter solstice, and from then on the Jews celebrated the victory with a new festival, the festival of lights called Chanukkah. So there you have another reason for Christians adopting this date for the birth of Christ, this new light of the world. Don't you think that interesting?"

"Is it? You don't want to try too hard to find rhymes and reasons for how things came about," Harry replied. "I like Christmas for what it is, not for where it came from," he said happily.

"You mean you like Christmas because of plum pudding and brandy butter?" I queried.

"That's one reason."

"You like Christmas for roast turkey and sprouts?"

"And why not?"

"Mince pies – Christmas cake?"

"Yes, of course!"

"Christmas presents – Christmas cards – Christmas tree?"

"Ummm. Gross waste of money!" Harry was beginning to remember the expense.

"Or do you like Christmas for going to church and hearing the vicar waffling about the miracle of it all from the pulpit?" I asked with a fine edge of sarcasm to my voice.

There was a polite cough behind me, and a louder cough and positive biff from Harry indicating that the Canon with his hangdog face and patient, somewhat cautious expression, was just behind me waiting for a suitable moment to interrupt. He was clearly accustomed to diverse views amongst his parishioners and had an air of kindly detachment. He told us that the others had already left the crypt and it was time to move on from there.

As he followed us up the steps he remarked pleasantly: "Many people forget that King David was born here in Bethlehem."

"Of course, so he was! Thank you for reminding us," I replied.

"As a boy, David watched over his father's sheep until God chose him to become King over all Israel," he went on.

"Was that why the Christmas story has shepherds watching over their sheep by night – a sort of King David link?" I asked.

"That may well be the case," came the calm reply.

"Which explains the hymn *Once in Royal David's City*?" I remarked.

"Indeed," the Canon said.

We came up into the body of the church where the Canon's wife was waiting for him. As they strolled off together I remembered that I'd read that David had also excelled in playing the harp, and in the night he would sing God's praises and study the Torah. God must have loved King David for his praise and worship of him. He was then told by God that he would die on the Sabbath, but which Sabbath wasn't revealed so that David worshipped and prayed each Sabbath in abundance for fear it might be his last. When he did die it was, as had been foretold, on the Sabbath.

At dinner that night I found myself seated between the Irish girl and Harry. We were at one end of the table with the Canon's wife at the other end, and an elderly Scottish woman seated across from us. Conversation was spasmodic, and the Irish girl seemed particularly silent and preoccupied when she suddenly turned to me and said: "When do you think the last bus leaves for Bethlehem?"

"For Bethlehem? Why?" I asked in surprise.

"Oh, I'd really like to go back there," she said.

"What, tonight?"

"Why not?"

"Well, how will you get back? And what do you want to do when you're there?"

"Oh, I'll manage," she said. For a while she ate in silence, then said: "I'd love to go back there. I just love Bethlehem!"

I noticed that the Canon's wife was watching and listening. "What is she wanting to do?" she enquired.

The Irish girl answered promptly: "I'd like to return to Bethlehem. When do you think the last bus leaves?"

The Canon's wife kept her cool and said: "You'll need your passport from the hotel security safe, and my husband has the receipt for them all. You'll have to get it from him."

"Why on earth would you be wanting to go to Bethlehem at this time of the night, pet?" enquired the elderly Scottish woman – I learned later she was eighty-seven.

"I don't know. I love Bethlehem, and I want to go back."

"Well, if you ask me," said the Scottish woman with all the power of age and wisdom behind her, "that's not just unintelligent, it's downright stupid!"

The Irish girl ignored her, finished her food, then rose from her chair without a word and left with her nose in the air and a purposeful look.

The Scottish woman shook her head sadly. "If you ask me there's something wrong with the lass," she said. "At lunch today she was up, down, up, down seven or eight times. There's something wrong there," she repeated, and she shook her head again and looked across at the Canon's wife who remained silent, her eyes following the Irish girl who was leaving the dining-room.

"Perhaps it's significant," I said to the Canon's wife, "that when we were going back to the coach in Bethlehem, there were two or three Arabs, and one of them called out that he'd give two hundred camels for her."

"Is that so, pet? And what did she say?" asked the Scottish woman.

"She didn't. But I asked him first to show us the camels."

The Canon's wife allowed herself the suspicion of a smile.

First thing the next morning I opened up my notebook and wrote: *Didn't sleep well, don't know why. At dawn I heard a hurried scampering of feet passing our door – Irish girl? Her room is next to ours. I wonder where she was last night? I can't believe she went to Bethlehem. I like her but she's decidedly odd – perhaps that's why I like her!*

Yesterday was a fascinating day. The Church of the Nativity was very mystical. Afterwards we were taken out of Bethlehem to what's known as the Shepherds' Fields, to the Church of the Angels. The Church of the Angels was dark and all very cave-like, designed to give an authentic feel that here the shepherds watched over their flocks and all that – I wonder why they watched and didn't sleep by night? I've never known any shepherd to watch over his sheep by night. He might go and help with a lambing, but not watch. Harry, when I made this point, said that of course they watched because there were wolves. But Michael said the sheep would have been brought in in winter.

As we're on a Christian pilgrimage a communion service was held in this cave-church taken by the Canon. The Canon has a certain presence in church where he comes into his own, and has a quiet authority. He looked so kindly disposed in his cream and gold vestments, and said the prayers in such a natural way (not sonorously or pompously or in a holier-than-thou way) that I felt very lamb-like and amenable and took communion along with the others. I was quite surprised at myself. As Harry keeps telling me I must act the part of a true pilgrim while out here, and toe the line to what's expected.

Today we're to visit more of Jerusalem including the Wailing Wall. That will be interesting!

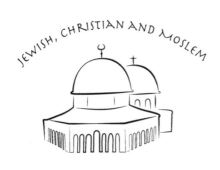

CHAPTER

3

JERUSALEM

Michael began to summon us, walking backwards with both arms raised to draw our attention. We were in the Upper Room where Jesus and his disciples had gathered for the Last Supper at the Jewish Passover, and where also the Holy Spirit had descended on the disciples when they were there together again fifty days later.

The Upper Room was a high, vaulted hall with Gothic arches and wasn't, in fact, the Upper Room at all but where it was thought to have been. In truth it was a twelfth century Crusader building which had later been converted to a mosque; it had bright blue and red stained-glass windows, a pulpit and a *mihrab* marking the direction of Mecca.

Michael informed us that in his opinion there was a slight discrepancy in St. Luke (Luke 22:10-13) regarding the reality of life at the time of Christ. He didn't think it could be right that for the Passover Jesus had told two of his disciples to follow a man carrying a water jug who would lead them to the house where they were to eat the Passover feast; in those days no man would have carried water, it was the duty of women to fetch water, he said.

The Scottish minister read a short passage from Acts which was appropriate to where we were.

"'When the day of Pentecost had come, they were all together in one place. And suddenly a sound came from heaven like the rush of a mighty wind, and it filled all the house where they were sitting. And there appeared to them tongues as of fire, distributed and resting on each one of them. And they were all filled with the Holy Spirit and began to speak in other tongues, as the Spirit gave them utterance.'" (Acts 2: 1-4).

"You know," I said to Harry afterwards, when we had been let loose to wander around to take photographs, "we think of the disciples as Christian, but they were, in fact, Jews who'd gathered in the Upper Room for their Jewish Shavuot festival."

"Jewish Shavuot. Hum." Harry eased himself down to a stone ledge. He had that morning woken up with lumbago, something which sometimes occurred when sleeping in a strange bed. He was finding it a struggle 'staying with it' as they say. I pressed on with my line of thought, hoping to take his mind off his problem: "Christians later called the Shavuot festival Pentecost because it was held fifty days after Passover. The word 'pentecost' is Greek for 'fiftieth' – seven sevens are forty-nine plus one equals fifty. Got it?"

"Got what?"

Harry's mind was anchored into his lumbago. For him it was quite irrelevant being in the Upper Room and recalling things from two thousand years ago when he was tethered to the present moment with his pain. I tried to show concern, though in truth I was much more interested in the past than his present problem. I pulled myself back from antiquity and attempted sympathy: "Poor you. Would you like to go back to the hotel?"

"What? Alone through all these alleyways? I'd never find it!"

"Well, I could come with you and then come back again," I said, playing the martyr.

"No, you'd never find it back either. I don't want you getting lost," Harry replied, also playing the martyr. "I expect I'll be all right," he said nobly. He took a pain-killer and gulped it down with water from his bottle.

We'd just come fom the Pool of Bethesda. There there'd once been a sanctuary of Asclepius, pagan god of healing (son of Apollo). Romans had come to be healed through the medium of this old pagan god. It was there also that Jesus had performed a miracle on a cripple. "'Rise, take up your pallet, and walk,"' Jesus had said, 'And at once the man was healed, and he took up his pallet and walked.' (John 5:8). Harry had had no miracle cure. He pinned his faith and hope on the pill he'd swallowed. I too, for that matter.

I left Harry, and wandered around. The first Jewish Shavuot festival had, apparently, been commanded by God in Deuteronomy, when Jews had been ordered to give gifts to him in thanks for their wheat harvest. After Christianity had taken off, the Jews had given a boost to their festival by shifting the emphasis from offering thanks for their wheat harvest, to commemorating the Holy Spirit of God descending to Moses on Mount Sinai when he received the commandments.

I could hear the W.I. woman saying: "Yes, I know it would! Not everyone has been in the Upper Room! I'll go and ask if she'd take us under that stained-glass window. Garish? Isn't it just! The sort of garish colours you'd expect in a mosque – eastern religion and all that."

She approached me cheerfully, her arm outstretched with her camera. "Would you mind? No need to pay attention to any of these knobs, just click on this thing." She busied herself with her small group, bunching them together, then called out from her central position: "Here we all are in the Upper Room! That's something we'll all remember!"

I took the photo.

The Canon's wife passed by, and her dragon-like expression softened as she caught my eye. She gave me one of her sweet smiles, and said: "Is Harry all right? He seems a little under the weather." I told her of his back trouble. "So painful," she said, then forgot about it. "To think that it all happened here! First Jesus, our Redeemer, eating the Passover feast with his disciples, and then the apostles and the Holy Spirit descending!" she murmured.

It was easy to imagine the scene in the Upper Room. It hardly mattered whether this was the actual room or not. Masterpieces of art have stamped themselves on the mind and made gospel stories a reality, such as, for instance, the Last Supper by Da Vinci, portraying the long table and the disciples seated at it with Jesus at their centre. So much has been imposed into the psyche by visual art; in fact, in the days when many were unable to read, art was an integral part of carrot and stick instruction where Christianity was concerned. Mosaics, frescoes and icons were designed to impress themselves on the human mind with visions of paradise, or of sinners being pitchforked into the flames of hell – the faith/fear syndrome.

We had to undergo tight security checks before being allowed through to the open space before the Western Wall, the last remaining wall of the original temple and commonly known as the Wailing Wall. As we came out from the security building a clamour of voices filled the air from the numerous Jews praying before the ancient stones.

Not so long ago this open space had been a maze of alleyways filled with small, tightly packed houses where over a thousand people, mostly Moroccan Arabs, had lived. At the end of the Six-Day War when the Israelis regained East Jerusalem from the Jordanians and with it this Western Wall, the generals on the spot had taken the instant decision to clear away the houses and create this open plaza in time for a Jewish festival to be held a few days later. The Moslem inhabitants had been given thirty minutes notice to quit before the bulldozers came in. By morning all the homes were gone and the area had been flattened. The regaining of these ancient stones had been considered by many Jews as divine providence and the will of God.

Here in the plaza, women and men had to separate, the men going to the left of a partition, and the women to the right. It was midday and bar mitzvahs were being held. There were several family gatherings, with dancing, feasting and the blowing of the shofar. Because men and women were involved, family parties were held at the top end of the plaza, well back from the partition fence.

Harry wasn't one to go down to the wall and put his forehead against a super-large block of stone to pray. I suspected he found this public display of religious fervour and spiritual outpourings very over-the-top. The English way of down-on-your-knees in silence was much more to his liking. I left him nursing his lumbago at the top of the plaza and joined the women.

They all had their heads covered, and a few sat poring over holy scripture while others stood rocking with their faces to the wall. I noticed the Irish girl with her mop of curly hair, her calf-length, straight cotton skirt, her pale bare legs in their wedged sandals, with her forehead against a block of stone. What was she praying for? During one of our conversations she'd declared her suspicion of men. "Never trust a man," she'd said. I'd told her she sounded as if she'd had a bad experience. "Oh, yes, I have," she'd admitted. But she hadn't elaborated.

Some women were standing on plastic chairs and peering over the partition at the men. I clambered onto a chair to take a look. Below on the men's side there were tables on which were leather-bound Torahs and suchlike holy books. I didn't know if they were being sold or were there like prayer-books to be borrowed for the occasion.

The scene reminded me of Jesus overturning the tables of the money-changers and the seats of those who sold pigeons, scolding everyone because they were not using the temple as God had intended but had turned it into 'a den of thieves'. I always thought his treatment somewhat harsh, especially since I'd learned that the money-changers were only there in order to change Roman coins (which bore the head of Caesar and would, therefore, profane the temple) into shekels, the only currency allowed inside the temple precincts. Those selling pigeons also were only there so the poor could purchase something to sacrifice, in this case a very humble offering.

Peering over the partition, I saw the men praying at the wall, all wearing skull-caps or black hats; some of them with sidelocks, and many rocking from the waist, forward and back, their faces to the wall.

The massive stones, which were all that remained of the Second Temple, reminded me also of Jesus' prophecy: "'...there will not be left here one stone upon another, that will not be thrown down...'" (Matthew 24:1-3). The destruction of the temple had come about in 70 A.D. In fact, this Wailing Wall wasn't really part of the temple itself but was a retaining wall built by Herod the Great when he renovated the Second Temple in a bid to popularize himself with the Jews. The massive stones were amazingly impressive – a honey-beige colour. The Romans hadn't wanted to destroy the temple but had been forced to do it when the Jews refused to surrender. It was the usual deadlock of human wills. With its final destruction the Jews either died in battle, were taken captive or fled.

In the second century, when the Emperor Hadrian rebuilt the city calling it *Aelia Capitolina,* only pagans and Christians were inhabiting the city and, in the fourth century A.D., when Constantine finally accepted Christianity as a true religion, many churches were founded by him and Christianity began to flourish.

Then, regarding Jerusalem as a desirable centre because it was where the trade routes crossed, Persia invaded the city in 614 A.D. It is believed that many Jews had joined the Persian army, seeing it as an opportunity to regain their homeland. When they finally overran Jerusalem, the Persians and Jews alike became like demented beings, ruthlessly and mercilessly slaughtering the inhabitants and looting, and destroying the churches. The returning Jews regarded it as history repeating itself because it had originally been the Persians who'd assisted them to return from their Babylonian exile those many centuries before. The Persian victory, however, was to be short-lived because soon the armies of Islam swept up from the south and drove them out.

I walked closer to the massive blocks of stone. Folded slips of paper containing prayers cascaded from crevices in the wall. Beyond the wall and out of sight was the Dome of the Rock built on the Haram al-Sharif, or Temple Mount as it is also called. It was built over the Rock where the original temple built by Solomon had stood until its destruction by the Babylonians, and the Second Temple until it too was destroyed by the Romans.

I was very conscious of being at the religious centre of the world, a focal point for Jews, Christians and Moslems. When the Israelites had first arrived in their 'promised land' the Canaanites had had their own deities, especially Baal. God, however, or Yahweh as the Jews called him, resolved matters by ordering a complete massacre of the Canaanites, and threatening his 'chosen' with a similar fate if they failed to obey and worship him, and him only.

And so Yahweh reigned supreme with occasional lapses when Baal did. But God sent prophets to admonish his 'stiff-necked' people, and warned them of dire consequences if they didn't mend their ways.

Isaiah had been one of the prophets living here in Jerusalem in the eighth century B.C. He had been a greatly respected figure and was the brother of King Amaziah of Judah. Amaziah's heir had been Hezekiah who'd married Isaiah's daughter, but their son, Manasseh (Isaiah's grandson) had turned against Isaiah, accusing him of being a false prophet. Isaiah had then fled from him, and had hidden in a tree, but he'd been spotted and his grandson had had the tree cut down so killing the unfortunate Isaiah.

In the fourth century B.C., following on from Alexander the Great's conquests, the Olympian gods had had their turn in Palestine. It was at that time that, horror of horrors, the altar to Zeus Olympius had been set up in the Jewish temple. The situation had lasted for about a century before the pious, priestly Maccabean family rose up in revolt, and the proper worship of Yahweh was restored in the temple. After that the Romans had come, which saw the dawning of Christianity. The Christians maintained that God miraculously conceived a son who was the long awaited Messiah. But, instead of freeing the Jews from Roman rule as had been the fervent hope of the Jews, he had been crucified instead.

Jews, guided by Yahweh (who was also the God of the Christians) were quite unable to accept the idea that Jesus had been their long awaited Messiah. Firstly, Jesus had made no attempt to overthrow the Roman occupation of Palestine and, secondly, Jews had God's commandment to worship him and him alone.

So where did God stand in all this?

I'd put the matter to Harry who'd merely said that God never got things wrong, only humans did, which really didn't help.

And Islam? Well, six hundred years later Allah (who was Yahweh to the Jews, and God to the Christians) enlightened Muhammad with the Koran. In it he made it clear that the Christians were mistaken because no way could Allah have a son. Jesus was a prophet. '...believe in God and His apostles and do not say: "Three." Forbear, and it shall be better for you. God is but one God. God forbid that He should have a son!' (Sura 4:171).

That was fascinating! Why hadn't God enlightened Christians with that knowledge from the start?

I grew tired of gazing at these massive gold-grey blocks of stone before me with the women beseeching or poring over the meaning of holy texts. My attention was drawn instead to a fat pigeon strutting along a ledge and entering between the bars of a small glassless window of a building on the right. At the time the pigeon seemed to me eminently sensible and at peace with life; he had no religious consciousness, but lived his pigeon life without any sense of the divine. Why were all these people standing at the wall apparently hooked up to an invisible deity? Was it all the result of the written word? Words said by many to be of such significance that no one was to question them? Words in the Old Testament versus those in the Gospels, versus other words in the Koran? Words which brought Jews to this Western Wall, Christians to the Church of the Holy Sepulchre, and Moslems to their Dome of the Rock?

The Moslem Dome of the Rock was tantalizingly close. It was supposed to have been part of our itinerary but we'd been told that it was considered unsafe to be taken up there, so the visit had been cancelled.

I returned to Harry who'd been watching the bar mitzvahs. Men and women were dancing in a circle, hands held loosely whilst a central figure blew a blast on the shofar, a long, harsh sound. The shrill ululating of the women sounded like a cross between demented singing and a Red Indian war cry.

Michael was pointing out to Harry some contraption on a building (I couldn't really see what) and telling him that in this age of technology Jews all around the world now sent emails to God. These were printed out, folded and inserted into crevices in the wall along with the other prayers. In this manner Jews, who were unable to travel to their holiest of holy cities, could feel in touch with their ancient religious roots wherever they were in the world.

Soon we were all being walked briskly through a narrow picturesque souq where I would have liked to have lingered, but instead was frog-marched in line with the others. I wondered what the vendors must be thinking seeing us tourists hurrying past with money enough to fly to Jerusalem but spending not a penny on their wares. They appeared indifferent, sitting patiently and resignedly awaiting a change to their fate and fortunes. If it was Allah's will that they should sit and not sell, so be it.

We ourselves were going to have lunch at the Ecce Homo Bienvenue Hostel in the heart of the old city. I felt mildly guilty, but pleased that for us anyway food was on the agenda.

I am up on the flat roof of the Ecce Homo Hostel building in the heart of Jerusalem. We've just had lunch and Harry's remained down below because of his lumbago.

I want to jot down some things before I forget, i.e. King David's tomb – a small oblong room which we visited briefly. In the room was his tomb/coffin covered with a black (I think velvet) cloth embroidered with gold emblems such as the Star of David, the harp and a crown. Placed on top were two silver-wrought cylindrical containers in which I presumed were sacred scrolls. Between them was a large lamp from which the light of Israel is said to go out to the world at large. A high-backed chair was against one wall and Michael told us the chair was awaiting Elijah's return. The Jews believe his return will herald the coming of their Messiah.

At their Pesach (Passover) celebrations Jews also have a cup of wine poured out for Elijah, and the door of every house is left open so that he is able to enter – it's said that Elijah visits every Jewish household at Pesach in order to give it his protection. Children are excited when they find some of the wine from Elijah's cup has gone (adults see to this) and they are told that yes, Elijah has visited. A sort of Father Christmas coming down the chimney magical story to delight children.

From this roof top there is a marvellous view out over

Jerusalem. When earlier I was standing by the parapet wall here I could see the Dome of the Rock resplendent in the early afternoon sun, and was able to glimpse its great forecourt where human beings the size of ants were to be seen wandering about. The Dome of the Rock is not a mosque for congregational worship, but a place for contemplation and prayer where visitors can stroll in silence, and pause in admiration at its tiled facade with its flowing Arabic script revealing verses from the Koran, and numerous intricate geometric designs in various shades of blues and yellow.

It's interesting that before Muhammad received his revelation, the Arabs living around Mecca were worshipping al-Llah at the Ka'bah, which even then was a holy shrine. Al-Llah was the pagan High God of Mecca who had three daughters, al-Uzzah, al-Lat and Manat, though they were thought to be divine presences to be acknowledged more than deities to be worshipped.

To go back to the Dome of the Rock, or rather to THE Rock under the Dome. When the Crusaders conquered Jerusalem they made some major alterations to convert the Dome to Christian use. They turned THE Rock into an altar, covered the Koranic verses with Latin texts, and put a cross on the top of the Dome. But then in the twelfth century Saladin recaptured the city and restored the Dome to Islam, replacing the cross with the crescent moon.

The importance of THE Rock is because it's believed to be the foundation stone on which the world was created. Rock is indestructible which is why it's of such significance. At the end of time it is believed the Black Stone from the Ka'bah in Mecca will unite with THE Rock under the Dome in a sort of religious grand finale.

So THE Rock is where the world began and where it will end. Interesting!

Oh, blow! I can see the Irish girl's pale legs and wedged sandals approaching...

"What are you writing? Is it a diary you're writing?"

"Oh, hello. I always jot down things so that I don't forget what we've seen."

"It's grand up here on the roof," she said.

"This is the nearest we'll ever get to the Temple Mount," I said, joining her at the parapet wall.

"I want to get up there," she said.

"Well, we've been advised against it."

"I don't think it's right to put it on our itinerary and then not to take us," she complained.

"Well, it's probably better to be safe than shot."

"Shot? Do you think so?"

I thought it best to be positive with one so volatile and impulsive. "They're trigger happy up there," I said.

She turned her head briefly towards me, was about to complain further, but changed her mind. "So why do they call it the Dome of the Rock, then?" she asked.

"It was on the Rock that Abraham was prepared to sacrifice his son, Isaac," I said.

"Is that so?"

"And also it was there they say Adam landed when he was cast out of the Garden of Eden by God. And it was from there that Muhammad made his Night Journey."

"His Night Journey? What was that, then?" She looked sideways at me. I didn't look at her but could imagine her grey eyes watching me warily.

"It's a nice story," I said. I glanced at my watch to check that time wasn't running out on us. We had ten minutes.

I told her how one night, when Muhammad was asleep in Medina where he'd been living since his flight from Mecca, the Angel Gabriel had appeared together with a shining beast, and had told Muhammad to climb up on the animal. This Muhammad had obediently done and off they'd set. Every stride had reached to the horizon so that in no time they'd arrived in Jerusalem at the Rock. At the Rock Gabriel told Muhammad to dismount and ordered him to go up through the seven heavens to God who wished to see him. I paused to give her time to digest this bit of information, then pressed on with the story. I told her how Muhammad had spoken with some of the prophets as he'd passed through one of the heavens, though what they'd said wasn't recorded.

"Probably about the sins of the world," said the girl.

"Or, maybe, about how good the world was considering all things?" I suggested.

"You think so?"

"Well – why not?"

"So what happened then?" asked the girl. And I told her how Muhammad finally reached God's presence. It wasn't certain whether he actually came face to face with Allah or whether it was his heart which had felt Allah's presence.

"So what did Allah say?" she asked.

"Allah told Muhammad that he must return to earth and see to it that his followers prayed fifty times a day."

"Did you say fifty?" I nodded. "And what did Muhammad say to that?"

"Well, he didn't argue," I replied. "But when he returned down through the heavens he met Moses again, and Moses was adamant that fifty times was unreasonable, and that Muhammad must return to God and ask him to reduce it."

"And did he?"

"Yes, he did."

"That was brave of him!"

"Very brave. So he went back and God agreed that forty would be all right."

"Forty! That's still unreasonable."

"That's what Moses said," I agreed. "He insisted that Muhammad return repeatedly until God reduced the number to five. And even that Moses thought too much, but by this time Muhammad had lost his nerve and refused to face God again."

"I like the story!" said the Irish girl.

We gazed over the roof tops to the numerous church domes bearing crosses, and the various minarets piercing through the huddled buildings, and to the broad grey dome of the Church of the Holy Sepulchre.

"Are you a Catholic?" I asked. I was always curious regarding other people's beliefs.

"Oh, yes, I am. And you?" she enquired, turning to look at me again.

"Mmmm. A sceptic?" I put it as a question rather than a statement as at any moment I might change.

"If you're a sceptic why have you come?" she asked.

"Because I find it interesting – fascinating, in fact."

"Aren't you afraid of hell?"

"Should I be?"

"If you don't believe in our Lord then you're damned," she said firmly. "You can't be happy, not if you don't believe in our Lord."

I was silent. I couldn't see why I should be distressed by my situation. I believed in a spirit, which was one third of the Trinity. If God of the Old and New Testament existed then he had only to make it evident beyond any doubt. I couldn't find the evidence in other people's declarations of belief. But maybe in the Church of the Holy Sepulchre where we were going that afternoon everything would change. I somehow felt that if it was ever to happen, that's where I would get my long awaited spiritual enlightenment.

I didn't feel mystical as I stood inside the Holy Sepulchre. Despite the candles and the sombre mystique, nothing spectacular occurred. The Greek Orthodox priest on duty was positively snappish about something, and it was catching. No doubt it was boring for him herding ecstatic or expectant pilgrims through one door (six at a time) and out through another – a tedious job and the quicker done the better. No time was allowed for any spiritual awakenings – not that time was needed as such revelations take split seconds. But my hoped-for vision or, at the very least, emotional awe and reverence, never materialised, and I came out feeling unexpectedly cross.

"Well, that's that," said Harry as he followed me out of the tomb. "Now what?"

I didn't know. We'd just been rushed around the Stations of the Cross along the Via Dolorosa and it had been difficult not to find the experience a total extinguishing of holy thoughts. Michael had fed us with titbits of information, such as the fact that we were going through what had once been the cheese market. He'd said that he liked to show pilgrims the Stations of the Cross when the souq was in full spate, as it gave a better picture of the indignity Jesus had had to endure when struggling under the weight of his cross going uphill along to Calvary.

At the Ninth Station of the Cross I'd seen three cats which had interested me more than the historical reasons over two thousand years earlier. The cats had been exciting because so far in Israel we'd seen no animals. I'd first noticed the lack of them in Bethlehem, and to see three cats at the ninth Station of the Cross had been quite stimulating.

"Look, three cats!" I'd said to Harry.

"Three cats? There must be rats – or mice," had been his immediate response.

Now standing in the Rotunda within which was the Holy Sepulchre, I told Harry how it was here that there'd once been a temple of Venus. It had been built by the Emperor Hadrian in 135 A.D. in honour of his new city which he'd called *Aelia Capitolina.*

"Don't you think that fascinating?" I said.

"Fascinating? Why?" His rest after lunch had eased his back and he was feeling attentive once again.

"Well, why would the Emperor Hadrian want to build a temple of Venus over the tomb of Jesus?"

"Haven't a clue," came the reply.

"Hadrian had tons of earth and rubble brought here, had it levelled off and laid a flagstoned platform on it for his new temple. He could have built it anywhere, but chose here. Why? Do you suppose it was because Venus was the goddess of love and it was a deliberate pagan statement of defiance against the new Christian conception of love?"

"Could be." Harry was non-committal.

"Then in three hundred and something when Constantine accepted Christianity as a true religion, he sent his mother, Helena, to spy out important landmarks in Jesus' life, and she learned that Christ's tomb was here beneath the temple of Venus. Or, perhaps, it was the other way about. Because there was a temple of Venus, Helena pinpointed the site to cock a snook at the pagan goddess of love and claim the site for the new Christian love? It could have happened that way?"

"Maybe."

"And as a wizard at finding lost Christian treasures, Helena also somehow miraculously discovered the cross on which Jesus was crucified," I said. "There are relics of the True Cross in hundreds of churches and monasteries, enough to build a ship," I added.

"Hum."

"Considering the cross was three hundred years old and had lain buried under rubble all that time, you'd have thought it would have disintegrated."

"Not if it was holy."

"In fact, it is said she found three crosses, two of which were the ones on which the thieves either side of Jesus were crucified. So two weren't holy crosses at all, and they hadn't crumbled either."

"Well, obviously there was something in the soil – "

"Rubble," I said.

"That preserved the wood."

"Three crosses, and the big question was which was the True Cross of Jesus?" I went on. "Easy. She had each cross held over a deceased woman and the corpse remained a corpse under the crosses of the two thieves, but sat up when the cross of Jesus was held over it. Remarkable?"

"Remarkable," Harry agreed.

"Unbelievable?" A rhetorical question.

"Perfectly believable since it was done with faith and devotion."

I regarded Harry critically for a moment. I hoped this pilgrimage wasn't bringing about some sort of religious awakening in him. I would find it difficult if he started beating a drum and singing hymns.

I remembered suddenly that the Holy Sepulchre was where the Easter Holy Fire ceremony was held annually.

I wanted to go back inside but it was now off-limits, and I wasn't going to face the snappy Orthodox priest a second time.

I was annoyed with myself for forgetting the Holy Fire while inside the tomb. It is considered a miraculous event that occurs always on the night of the Greek Orthodox Easter Resurrection service. The custom is for the Patriarch to enter the Holy Sepulchre alone where he prays. He has no way of lighting his 'Light of the world' symbol; but always and without fail fire comes down from heaven and hey presto, his candle is lit, and he then passes the flame through a hole in the wall to those waiting outside.

At the Easter Resurrection service there is always a crush of people wanting to see this spectacle. It is considered a sign from heaven, an unexplained phenomenon performed by the Holy Spirit or by Christ or God.

Robert Curzon, in his 1849 travel book *Visits to Monasteries in the Levant* said that the Armenian Patriarch had confided to him that it was a trick performed annually by the Greek Orthodox Patriarch who had to keep on with it because Christians, after all these centuries, were not to have their unshakable belief in it shattered.

We were summoned on to another part of this great building, to an area which had about it an aura of lofty grandeur and antiquity. I found myself standing beside the Scottish minister. "This is where they say Adam is buried," he said. He rubbed his hands together with an air of stating something which wasn't to be taken literally.

"I thought Adam was buried in Mecca?" I remarked. It was a wild guess, but as Adam and Eve had met again in Mecca after two hundred years of separation (so one story goes) so, I supposed, they had eventually died and been buried there.

"Och aye, he's no doubt buried there too. And you'll find he's buried at Hebron also, if I recall aright."

There were in this basilica church wonderful ancient columns and Michael pointed out one marking the actual spot where it was believed Christ had been crucified. He then indicated (I thought almost apologetically) cracks in a rock which were claimed to have been caused by the earthquake which had occurred at Jesus' death. '...and the earth shook, and the rocks were split...' (Matthew 27:51).

When I'd read about the crucifixion in the Gospel of Matthew it had struck me as significant that the centurion, who had been keeping watch over the tomb with several others, had witnessed the earthquake and had remarked that clearly Jesus must have been 'the Son of God'. But in my revised standard version of the Bible in an explanatory note it said 'the Son of God' could equally be 'a son of god' (the 's' and 'g' were not capital letters). To a Roman 'a son of god' would have been amazing but quite plausible as pagan gods were not averse to taking mortal women who gave birth to immortal sons. In fact, in the early days of Christianity, the Greeks and Romans had thought that Jesus was a new Olympian god.

Presumably the pagan deities, whom the early Christian Fathers were eager to condemn as non-gods, but mere statues and of no consequence, had really not been as powerless as Jews and Christians would have liked people to believe. The pagan gods had guided men perfectly well for several thousand years and, under their influence, whether the gods were mere 'poetic fancy' (as the Christian Fathers maintained) or not, men had developed a good system of justice, democracy, family loyalty and even, thanks to Socrates in the fifth century B.C., the idea that love was the greatest virtue men could strive after.

To read *The Iliad* was to discover to what excellence the Greeks aspired, and the achievements they'd accomplished under their Olympian gods. Men in those days prayed to them – to any one of the twelve – choosing the god or goddess most likely to bestow the help needed under a particular circumstance. If it was wisdom and justice required, then men prayed to the great goddess Athena; if marriage, then to Hera, goddess of marriage; if agriculture, then to Demeter, goddess of corn, and so on.

The early Christian Fathers in their condemnation of the pagan gods, had explained away men's surprisingly good track-record under pagan god guidance, by saying that it had been God Almighty working through these false gods. They never for a moment suggested it might be men themselves working their own human wills, the strongest amongst them picking their way through the forest of other wills.

I found it curious also that there had been twelve Olympian gods, twelve signs of the zodiac, twelve tribes of Israel and twelve disciples. Twelve seemed to be another mystical number.

I remembered that somewhere nearby there was a Moslem corner in honour of the caliph Umar who had captured Jerusalem in 637 A.D. It marked the spot where Umar had first prayed to Allah here in Jerusalem. I went and asked Michael who examined my face in a remote pondering-of-other-things manner. He probably wondered why I was thinking of Umar and not Jesus.

"In a minute, I will show you," he said.

Umar had become the second caliph. He hadn't always been an admirer of Muhammad and, whilst in Mecca, had at first been violently opposed to him and had set out to kill him. One day, however, he'd heard the Koran being read aloud, and had been so captivated by its poetic beauty that, instead of murdering Muhammad, he'd had an instant conversion.

When the Christian Patriarch, Sophronius, had surrendered the city to the Moslems, he had asked for Umar himself to come to meet him. This Umar had done and they'd met on the Mount of Olives where the caliph (so it was reported) came wearing threadbare clothes and riding on an ass, so fulfilling the same prophecy in Zechariah (Zechariah 9:9) which Christians asserted Christ had fulfilled. In fact it was said that some Jews at that time thought that the caliph Umar coming in this manner might well be their long awaited Messiah, until time in due course proved otherwise.

Michael pointed briefly to a minaret as we came out. "Umar's mosque," he said.

"Who's Umar?" Harry asked. I told him.

"Fulfilling Zechariah's prophecy, my foot!"

I didn't react to his sarcasm but wondered why, if the Christians could claim to have fulfilled prophecy, Moslems shouldn't also?

Soon we were again being marched through a souq.

"Where are we going?" asked the Irish girl hurrying up alongside me.

"I don't know," I replied.

"To the Garden Tomb..." put in the Canon's wife. She was breathless as she struggled to keep up with everyone. Her heavy bulk was a hindrance even though her mind soared like a bird: "It's quite possible that our Lord's crucifixion took place there... Sorry, must catch my breath..." Catching her breath meant keeping up the pace without speaking.

I could hear ahead of us the voice of the W.I. woman: "Look at those spices! – Oh, postcards! but we can't stop. –

What a selection of nuts! Yes, ain't they just! – underwear! – scarves!"

It was a narrow, picturesque souq where I would have liked to have lingered and browsed.

The W.I. woman's voice continued unabated: "...I suppose it's a sort of spinach? Looks a bit wilted to me – I can't tell without stopping and we're not allowed to it seems! I suppose they come in from some village with their produce – that looks like mint – and sit all day hoping for custom – wouldn't want to be them! – Who would want to buy that meat there, the flies! – Oh, wouldn't I just, I could really do with a hat! I've a wedding coming up – copper – saucepans – aspirin."

We all came to a standstill suddenly and had to step aside as a young boy came down the alleyway with a hand-cart piled high with toilet rolls. They were at a precarious angle and about to topple off; poor little chap couldn't see where he was going and the load was running away with him on a downhill zigzag course.

With him safely past, the W.I. woman's voice continued: "Books! Oh, they might just have – yes, in English – but we can't browse, not allowed to browse – and C.Ds! – Radios and computers! Photographic equipment! – Oh, I must stop! – Gourds! Talk of Alladin's Cave! – Jewellery! All those beads and brooches and rings! – By heavens, what haven't they got! – Drums and guitars! – Sweets! Very suspect, dear, I wouldn't buy them for my grandchildren. – Hookahs! – Carpets! – Pyjamas! – Melons! You name it and they've got it, haven't they just!"

That night I scribbled my thoughts for the day in my notebook:

After a whole day in Jerusalem nothing magical has happened – no awakening, no sudden revelation, not a spark of understanding. If anything rather the reverse.

We walked to the Garden Tomb from the Damascus Gate where we spent about an hour listening to an irritating Englishman who told us he'd found Jesus. The garden itself had trees, shrubs, and a few flower beds. From odd corners of it came strumming guitars and voices singing Alleluyia-type songs. Our guide told us how he'd come to the Garden Tomb on holiday twelve years ago in order to help out for a few weeks, but 'the good Lord' had had other ideas for him and he had been there ever since.

He told us how General Gordon of Khartoum first noticed the rocky hill in 1883 with its two caves for eyes which resembled a skull. Somehow the idea took off that this was a more likely place for Jesus to have been crucified and buried. In John's gospel (19:17) it says 'So they took Jesus, and he went out bearing his own cross to the place called the place of the skull, which is called in Hebrew Golgotha.' Presumably the sentence 'And he went out bearing his own cross...' meant 'went out of the city'. An advert was placed in the Times to raise money to purchase General Gordon's 'place of the skull' and money was quickly raised, and it was bought by the Anglican Church. I've read somewhere that, in fact, the whole 'place of the skull' idea was a ploy by the Church of England (jealous of the Catholic monopoly of churches in Jerusalem) to acquire its own corner for pilgrims.

As it was the end of a long day I think the man found us somewhat wanting and not as attentive as he would have liked. He kept asking us questions, such as: "So where was Jesus crucified?" And when there was no answer he'd slap his thigh with a small cane he carried. "Right here in this garden!" He always replied to his own questions. "What does Golgotha mean?" *Slap, slap* as he waited. "'The place of the skull'!" We were all seated on a line of benches at the top of the garden. "And where is Golgotha?" *Slap, slap.* "Here outside the city walls!" "So where did Joseph of Arimathea have his family tomb?" Many of us had our eyes shut while we rested. *Slap.* "Right here at Golgotha!"

We were taken to see the tomb itself, a small stone structure built against the rocky hill. It had a low entrance which would have been sealed after the burial of a body, and high up a small opening through which the soul could fly out. We were allowed inside, two at a time. "And what did you find in the tomb?" *Slap, slap of the thigh.* "A notice! A notice saying 'He is not here'! And why is he not here?" *Slap, slap, slap, slap.* "Because our Lord was risen from the dead!" His statement was reinforced by the strumming of a guitar, and a voice from beyond the shrubbery singing: 'Jesus lives! Halleluyia!'

I think Jerusalem is curing me of religion altogether. I didn't expect that!!! Oh, well.

CHAPTER

4

QUMRAN AND MASADA

As we drove through the desert heading for Qumran, I was bewitched by the desolate grandeur of the scenery. We passed Bedouin with their flocks of sheep and goats. We were given snippets of information regarding Bedouin life. The women fetched the water whilst men sat around sipping coffee. A stranger would be welcomed with coffee, and a bed would be prepared and a pair of pyjamas set out for the guest.

"I'd never put on pyjamas belonging to a Bedouin," Harry declared positively.

"Well, if you were lost in the desert you'd be glad of anything," I countered.

"I'd stay in my own clothes, thank you," he said.

The Judaean wilderness was exotic in its own desert way. We were passing high sandy hillocks. As we drove past another flock of sheep we were informed that sheep in the heat of the day gathered together and lowered their heads as though in a rugger scrum, this way they sheltered themselves from the midday sun.

Soon we passed a signpost to Jericho. We could

glimpse the city and I wished we could do a quick detour to it. Jericho was the city where Joshua (whom Moses appointed leader of the Israelites at his death) was told by God to get his men to march around the city accompanied by his priests blowing 'trumpets of rams' horn'. They were to do this for six days and on the seventh day to do the same, but on the long trumpet call everyone was to shout and the walls would fall flat. This they obediently did – though why God had to put them through this marching and blowing of trumpets when he could as easily have seen to the walls collapsing without it, I couldn't understand.

"It's just a story," said Harry when I put my view to him on the subject. "A question of believing in the power of God."

"Well, yes. But that's my point. Why couldn't God have flattened the city walls without his poor Jews having to go those extra miles marching round and round the city?"

"A good lesson to everyone. Exert yourself to the limit and God will help if you obey his commands."

We passed low humps of Cappadocian-like tuffaceous rock in a whitish beige sandstone. We had to stop at a check-point but were allowed to pass without any problem. To our right there was an oasis with palm trees, beyond which was a backdrop of mountains. On our left was the Dead Sea, looking like ordinary sea with nothing dead about it. Beyond the Dead Sea, and seen only through a haze, were the mountains of Moab where Abraham had died.

We took a right turn and headed for some trees and buildings in their lonely expanse of white desert sand with rugged, same-coloured mountains looming beyond. High up on a rockface was the dark mouth of a cave. We were coming in to Qumran, site of the ascetic monastic settlement founded by the Essenes. They were a sect who first emerged around 150 B.C. as a result of the Hellenizing of the Jews and the subsequent Maccabean Revolt.

These ultra-Orthodox Jews had taken themselves off to the desert to keep the purity of the Jewish faith whilst awaiting the imminently expected Messiah. The Essenes were devoutly obedient to God's every whit and whim and observed his holy law meticulously as it had been given to Moses. But in 68 A.D. the Romans had come and destroyed the place and the community had scattered. Paganism had triumphed. Before fleeing, however, the sect had hidden their sacred texts in terra-cotta or stone jars in impossible-to-reach caves. They must have been very agile to have been able to clamber like goats up mountain-sides carrying tall clay pots with them.

The Dead Sea Scroll discovery had been the greatest manuscript haul since the findings at Nag Hammadi in Egypt two years earlier. The first scrolls at Qumran had been discovered in 1947, the year before the founding of the State of Israel, which many Jews regarded as a wonderfully good omen.

Here at Qumran we were first taken to the museum where we were given time to look at some of the exhibits. I found the ancient Hebrew script written on parchment or animal skin enthralling. There was something exotic about them and I wanted to unlock the mysteries they presented. Other items on display were things such as writing materials: pens made from bamboo used by the scribes, clay inkwells, oil lamps and so on. There was a long white marble table, its length determined by the size of the longest scroll when laid out flat. Apparently one scroll of Isaiah was over eight metres in length.

We went out to look at the ruined walls of the settlement which included water cisterns and a purification bath. We were told that every time the word 'God' had been either mentioned or written then the Essene had had to take a purifying bath. Really? They must have been perpetually jumping into the water. I wondered whether, when the weather was really hot, they'd been tempted to mention the word 'God' deliberately in order to take yet another cooling dip.

But it was a frivolous thought. This was a seriously dedicated religious community. No one with such a turn of mind would have ever been admitted to the fraternity. Michael went on to say that the purification bath had required moving water for true sanctification. Rain water was precious and when it rained it hopefully would fill the cisterns, and it was also brought to the site by aqueduct from the hills and channelled into the settlement.

"I'd love to be a Hebrew scholar," said the Irish girl coming up beside me. "I'd like to be able to decipher ancient texts."

"Well, you'd better start studying," I said.

"Oh, I've started," she replied. "I've been learning for a year."

"Really?"

"I'd like to go to university and study ancient Hebrew," she said.

"Then you should."

"Do you think so?" She gave me a two second scrutiny to see if I was serious.

"Certainly."

"Then maybe I will. Maybe I'll do it."

Forgetting her Roman Catholicism, and at that moment thinking of her as academic, I foolishly said: "I've read that one of the scholars working on the scrolls was a Dominican priest who concealed for years – in fact for decades – his findings, in order not to upset the Catholic Church."

"Who told you that?" she demanded.

"Where did I read it, you mean? Well, it was reported by various non-Catholic scholars," I replied.

"Oh, but they would, wouldn't they! You shouldn't believe what unbelievers say," she said.

"I suppose not," I remarked, trying to keep the conversation on an even keel, but then I added: "Though it's not exactly right for the Roman Catholic Church to insist that scholars should only report archaeological discoveries which conform to their own Church doctrine."

"Oh, that's just rubbish!" she said. She regarded me briefly, was about to say something more but turned away abruptly and was gone to do a circuit of the purification bath with its flight of cracked steps leading down into it.

I wandered on among the ruins feeling somewhat bemused by the desolation, when suddenly the Irish girl was beside me again.

"What else have you read?" she demanded.

Maybe I quite enjoyed seeing her fierce reactions as I told her about the Habakkuk Commentary which referred to the 'Teacher', the 'Liar' and the 'Wicked Priest'.

"Some scholars identify the 'Teacher' as James, the brother of Jesus, who insisted on obedience to the law," I told her. "And the 'Wicked Priest' was, or so they suggest, the High Priest, Ananias. As for the 'Liar', they suggest he was – " I stopped.

"Who was the 'Liar'?" demanded the Irish girl, her nose in the air quivering as she sniffed the scent of heresy.

"It doesn't matter – I've forgotten," I replied.

"Oh, that I don't believe! Who was he?" she demanded.

"It's only speculation – scholarly speculation."

"So?"

"St. Paul," I said.

"St Paul was never a liar! It was St. Paul who brought the Lord Jesus Christ to the gentiles!" she said.

Harry joined us and remarked that in his opinion Qumran was one of the most God-forsaken ruins he'd ever seen. And he chose this moment to dump a great squib into the Irish girl's inflammable store of Christian doctrine and remarked: "It makes much more sense that the road to Damascus refers to here."

"What do you mean by that?" asked the Irish girl at once.

"There's a theory – well, there's a scroll called 'The Damascus Document' my wife was telling me about which refers to the Land of Damascus. You tell her," said Harry, passing the squib to me.

"Yes, what is the theory?" demanded the Irish girl.

"Hm." I gathered my thoughts, trying to separate explosive material from non-explosive, but couldn't do it. "Well, some people argue that when St. Paul had his blinding vision on the road to Damascus he was on his way here – here being known as the Land of Damascus – he wasn't going to Damascus in Syria."

"That's stupid!" said the Irish girl at once.

"It's only a theory," I said soothingly.

"It's a stupid theory!" she said. "Why would they say that?"

"Oh, only because no High Priest in Jerusalem would have dared give Paul authority to seize Christians in Syria which at the time was a separate Roman province. It would have caused a rumpus and threatened his own position in Jerusalem."

"Well, that doesn't prove it was here either, so it's very

stupid to suggest any such thing!" And the Irish girl could stand no more and marched off, this time to view the Judaean desert from the watch-tower.

We ourselves walked to the ruins of the refectory where the Essenes had once gathered for their communal meals. These were eaten in silence. The Essenes at Qumran were very strict in the matter of leadership and the seating at table. They'd held feasts similar to the Last Supper celebrated by Jesus. In the sect's 'Manual of Discipline' (the Community Rule) was the following: '...when the table has been prepared... the Priest shall be the first to stretch out his hand to bless the first-fruits of the bread and new wine'. Or in another text in the 'Messianic Rule' was: 'they shall gather for the common table, to eat and to drink new wine... let no man extend his hand over the first fruits of bread and wine before the Priest... thereafter, the Messiah of Israel shall extend his hand over the bread.' It was all fascinating stuff. The idea had been put forward that Jesus and his disciples had been Essenes, and Jesus had played out the role expected of the Messiah. It was just as well I hadn't mentioned that to the Irish girl.

I really liked her for all her peculiarities. Apart from studying Hebrew I knew she spoke a bit of Arabic because I'd seen her asking a rather handsome looking Palestinian at reception to help her read a short text in Arabic. She'd held both hands with the fingers bent over the text like a hamster as she'd followed the letters and tried them out phonetically. The receptionist had had his head bent close to her mop of curly hair and had made cooing noises of encouragement. A queue of hotel guests had been waiting for attention but neither she nor he had been aware of them.

"Sh...wow...shu...k...ra...n – Shukran!"

"That's right! Shukran! Wellll donnnne! And this word?"

"A...l...h..a..ha...m...da...li...ll...a...h – Alham..."

"Yes – yessss – "The receptionist had waited expectantly and had been rewarded as the girl had announced triumphantly: "Al hamdalillah!"

"Wellll donnne! Now you speak Arabic!" He'd raised his head and had noticed the queue patiently waiting. He'd smiled charmingly at the guests and had said ingratiatingly to the Irish girl: "I will help you another time."

"There's another word here," the Irish girl had persisted, oblivious of the queue.

"We will speak every day!" the handsome receptionist had assured her, looking beyond her at what by now was an extensive queue. The girl had turned and had seen his problem.

"Oh, there are people waiting."

"Soooo gooood!" he'd cooed. "We try every day. It will be a pleasure!"

The Canon's wife pointed out to me the outline of the Roman camps far below in the desert as our cable-car carried us up to the top of Masada. Masada was an amazing, more or less sheer-sided flat-topped elevation in the middle of the desert about thirty miles south of Qumran. Herod the Great, when he became king of the Jews, used Masada as his desert retreat. He loved building and architecture and had, presumably, enough slave labour at his disposal to dig and quarry, heave and hoe and build this get-away-from-it-all palace fortress.

It was rough terrain on the summit and we were warned to watch our step as we followed in the wake of

Michael in his small navy sun-hat.

The Canon's wife was saying: "It's hard to imagine the Zealots holding out against the Romans for all those years!" She was red in the face from the midday heat and a little breathless. She picked her way carefully over the uneven ground as we trailed along behind the group. I offered her water from my bottle, and in general paid heed to what she was saying as she was keen on Roman history.

Michael was waiting for us stragglers and I noticed that the Irish girl, who'd been marching way off course, was now homing in on us again. We were told we were within the inner walls where the houses had been.

Many Zealots had taken possession of this desert fortress at the beginning of the First Jewish Revolt in 68 A.D. when they somehow managed to overpower the small Roman garrison there, and had subsequently held it for five years. Food? Well – they grew their own or had enough in store or, what was far more likely, survived by plundering and ravaging the locality. Water? Herod had seen to that by making large water cisterns (in truth, anyone but he himself had). They were quarried from this massive rockface and were supplied by the natural seasonal deluges. If you were born into the right strata of society then you drank and bathed, if you weren't then you probably died of dehydration as you quarried away to get the supply of water for the king and his entourage.

The Zealots had always hated Herod because he was not of pure Jewish stock. Equally, they refused to treat any Roman emperor as a god. So when they isolated themselves here at the start of the First Jewish Revolt (by which time Herod had been long dead) their instincts had been to fight to the death against the Romans. Not that God exactly helped them overpower the Roman emperor. Well, he helped them to hold out for five years, I supposed. The Jews believed that God was seeing to it that the Romans were being made complete asses of as the Roman general found it necessary to deploy a huge army to overpower the few. God even (and it was called a miracle, though a very minor one for God) changed the direction of the wind when the Romans catapulted up fire-brands to ignite the wooden beams in the defence walls. When they did this they'd made sure the wind was in the right direction, but it suddenly changed and sent the flames back towards them, threatening to incinerate and destroy their newly constructed siege towers. That indeed had been God's will, the Zealots declared at once, and were elated. But in no time the wind changed direction again and then it was the turn of the Romans to feel their gods were favouring them.

In fact all the Zealot courage and fortitude and trust in God couldn't compete with Roman military superiority. After a prolonged and wearying onslaught, the Romans finally managed to squash these Zealot gnats who were proving so obstinate.

It was, apparently, on the first day of Passover that the Zealots, rather than surrender, decided to commit mass suicide and deliver themselves up to God in preference to becoming slaves. There were just under a thousand men, women and children who died voluntarily, trusting in the hereafter and believing it was God's will that this was what they should do. Each man embraced his wife and stabbed her at the same time (and, presumably, his children) and then by drawing lots they killed each other till, finally, the rebel leader Eleazar ben Ya'ir turned his sword on himself.

The Herodian walls had to be admired. They were constructed with pentagonal shaped blocks of stone filled in between with smaller ones. His palace (no longer to be seen in its former splendour) had been a sort of hanging palace built on a series of terraces, and there had been a defence wall around the summit of Masada with no less than thirty-eight towers.

We arrived at Herod's bath. Nice warm water piped in from somewhere – lots of firewood heaved up, chopped up, put in place and set alight to heat the water. A good life for some. Even the roof had been domed so that steam didn't drip on to the pampered bathers, but ran down the sides back into the warm water.

We moved on and came to the Jewish Mikveh (the ritual bath) near to one of the oldest synagogues in the world. We were told by Michael that here in the synagogue ancient Hebrew scrolls had been found hidden in the walls. Jews never destroyed their Holy Scripture but concealed it from the enemy. Some Qumranic scrolls had also been found here.

"Do you have any questions?" Michael asked.

The Canon said: "I'd like to add that here beneath the floor of the synagogue some verses out of Ezekiel were buried. If we have time I'd like to read the passage out loud – Ezekiel 37:12-14." He glanced at Michael who gave a nod of assent. "It is Ezekiel's vision of a valley filled with bones, all of which God has said will live again." I supposed this must refer to the Jewish cemetery in the Kidron Valley. Or could Ezekiel have been prophesying about the bones of those who would be committing mass suicide? The Canon opened a marker in his Bible and found the place.

"'Therefore prophesy, and say to them, Thus says the Lord God: Behold, I will open your graves, and raise you from your graves, O my people; and I will bring you home into the land of Israel. And you shall know that I am the Lord, when I open your graves, and raise you from your graves, O my people. And I will put my Spirit within you, and you shall live, and I will place you in your own land; then you shall know that I, the Lord, have spoken, and I have done it, says the Lord.'" The Canon closed the Bible with a quietly sad expression.

The Scottish minister said: "The Zealots trusted in the good Lord and no doubt they were all resurrected."

"What happened to Masada afterwards?" asked the Irish girl. "What happened then? Was it deserted afterwards?"

"Yes, that is a good question," the Canon remarked. "In 132 A.D. there was the Second Jewish Revolt led by another Zealot called Simeon bar Kochba. His name means 'Son of the Star'. In the Book of Numbers, chapter 24, verse 17, it says: 'a star shall come forth out of Jacob.'"

"That wouldn't be anything to do with the star of Bethlehem, would it?" asked one of the Scottish women.

"Why would it be?" demanded the Irish girl defensively.

Michael eyed her solemnly, possibly assessing something of the Zealot in her: "Not that I am aware of," he said guardedly.

"Though the Star is mentioned in the War Rule Book amongst the Dead Sea Scrolls," said the Scottish minister. "It's not unreasonable to make a connection."

"You think there's a connection?" asked the Irish girl, on the attack at once.

"I only say it's not unreasonable to make a connection," he answered cautiously.

We tramped around and came finally to the remains of a fifth century Byzantine chapel. For Christian ascetics wanting to get away from worldly turmoil, such a Judaean desert retreat was ideal. But it was finally abandoned when the Moslems overran Palestine. The Moslems rather sensibly left Masada alone, recognizing it as an impossibly-hard-to-survive-on natural fortress stuck out alone in the desert, and a total bother to maintain.

"Well, I enjoyed that," said the Canon's wife collapsing onto a seat in the cable-car which was to take us back down. From it we watched two ant like figures far below making the ascent on foot along what was known as the Snake Path because it twisted and turned like a serpent.

Masada had, in fact, become a place of pilgrimage for young Jews who were taught to regard the Zealots of the past as legendary heroes. Today's young Israeli army recruits come up the Snake Path to Masada's summit for what is called a bonfire oath ceremony, in which they pledge to defend their land, the modern State of Israel, to the death. Today also school children, scouts and youth movements make it a point of honour to celebrate the glory of their Jewish forebears in an annual hike to the top of Masada. The time chosen for this celebration is Chanukkah (the Festival of Lights).

Many Israeli flags flew from Masada, both on the summit and down below. It was a place that symbolized all the ideal qualities needed to overcome the enemy, these qualities being courage, pride, fortitude and endurance.

It was late afternoon and the Dead Sea was now on our right as we drove back to Jerusalem. Gaza must have been fifty or so miles away to our left. I would have liked to have gone to Gaza, but Harry would never have agreed.

Our bag of medication would be a pathetic joke were we to get caught up in crossfire or shelling in the present Israeli/Palestinian conflict, or were we to be taken hostage. I wondered how I'd stand up to a kidnap. I suspected I would start with a grandiose show of bravado, until I got my first slap across the mouth. I'd find it incredibly difficult to cope with people who were full of hate, and didn't respond to my attempts to be friendly.

Situated as it was between Egypt and the Middle East, Gaza's history had always been one of conflict. Recognizing its strategic position, Alexander the Great had been stubbornly determined to capture the ancient Philistine city of Gaza which lay two miles inland on a high *tell* (the Arabic word for a hill resulting from layers of earlier civilizations). Apparently, Alexander had been advised by his engineers that it would be impossible to take the city perched on its *tell*, but to Alexander it was just another challenge, an obstacle to be overcome. To him the solution was quite obvious; if the city was on too high an elevation to make attack feasible, then the ground outside must be raised to the same level, and tunnelling under the walls would also help bring the city down. Amazingly, he achieved his objective, and the city was taken.

According to Josephus, the first century Jewish historian, in his *Antiquities of the Jews,* after capturing Gaza Alexander went up to Jerusalem. The High Priest of the day had been greatly alarmed assuming that Alexander was approaching as an enemy. But the High Priest had a dream in which God let him know that he need not fear Alexander but rather he should celebrate his arrival, and 'adorn the city, and open the gates' and go out to meet the warrior. This the High Priest did, accompanied by the citizens of Jerusalem, together with his fellow priests decked out in their priestly robes. Alexander, for his part, was highly flattered by the spectacle of the High Priest and the Jewish multitude coming out to meet him. He even (according to Josephus) went up into the temple and offered sacrifice to the Jewish God.

The result of Alexander's conquest of Gaza, however, was the building of temples there in honour of the Olympian gods, and these were to remain until the fourth century A.D. when Constantine the Great finally gave the nod of approval to Christianity.

In due course Gaza was left behind and we drew level with the town of Hebron also on our left. I wished we could do a detour to Hebron too (less than forty miles away) to see the Tomb of the Patriarchs. There Abraham was buried along with Isaac, Jacob, Sarah, Rebecca and Leah – and maybe Adam.

I wanted to visit the Haram al-Khalil, the Tomb of the Patriarchs. It was there in 1994 that Barukh Goldstein, an anti-Arab extremist, believed it was God's divine will that he should open fire on Moslem worshippers during their dawn prayers. It had been the Jewish festival of Purim, a day in which Jews celebrated their victory in the fifth century B.C. over their Persian enemies. It had been thanks to Esther, a Jewess who, without admitting her Jewish identity, had married the king of Persia. Amidst courtly tribulations and intrigues, she had consequently discovered a plot by the king's chief minister to wipe out all the Jews. Esther had pleaded with the king who had then decreed that all Jews should do the killing instead. For Goldstein (this modern day fanatic) Purim had been a heaven-sent day for his massacre. He'd managed to kill twenty-nine Moslems, and injured many more. He himself had then been beaten to death by the outraged Moslem congregation.

"Remember Goldstein?" I asked Harry.

"Should I?"

"He massacred a lot of Moslems in the Mosque of the Patriarchs in Hebron in 1994."

"Oh, him."

"Yes, oh, him. He's regarded as a Jewish martyr and, believe it or not, he's now a saint – Saint Barukh. How screwed up can that be to make a saint out of a mass murderer. Fundamentalists adore him and he has a wopping great tomb in one of the nearby settlements to which Jews come as pilgrims to beseech him to intercede on their behalf between them and God. And, apparently, Israeli settlers and soldiers in Hebron have now built a road for use only by Israelis. Yes, only by them! right bang through the Palestinian cemetery. And they've scrawled filthy graffiti on walls to offend them. It's really despicable. And do you know that some fundamentalist rabbi once said that he thought Arabs should be used for medical experiments?"

"Keep your voice down," Harry mumbled.

I thought it was down, but lowered it to *pianissimo*. "It's horrible to think that that family on the flight were Haredim fundamentalists. They appeared so nice. Yet they must have held extremist views."

"Say again? I can't hear you."

I tried not to shout. "As Haredim Jews they, no doubt, approved Goldstein's actions. I hate to think of that sweet little three year old being impregnated with his parents' fanatical beliefs and intransigence. Such people believe Arabs should be exterminated. They regard the murder of an Arab as not breaking God's commandment but as doing his will."

"I wouldn't mind a boiled sweet if you have one."

A boiled sweet? Here we were discussing mass murder and a sainthood for the murderer, and Harry was asking for a boiled sweet!

Oh, well.

I found the tin and opened it up for him and said: "The fact that the Moslems were in the middle of Ramadan at the time of Goldstein's murder I suppose is neither here nor there. All part of the greater mystery of God's divine plan," I remarked, no longer caring who overheard me.

"Good lemon flavour," said Harry who was enjoying his boiled sweet more than listening about Goldstein. "Hope we've more?"

But I wasn't going to let him get away with that!

"It was just the same with Yitzhak Rabin, the Israeli Prime Minister, who was assassinated by a wild fanatic Talmudic scholar because he was holding peace talks with the Palestinians."

"You have a boiled sweet," Harry offered. He clearly wasn't going to get into a discussion about fundamental Jews. "Personally I'd go for the bitter rather than the raspberry," went on the authority on boiled sweets who had by now reached the stage of being able to crunch his.

By now the road was winding through huge, off-white sandy hummocky hills, and my attention was drawn to this amazing desert scenery as the road twisted and turned on a gradual uphill gradient. We were heading for the heights above the Wadi Qelt to view the Greek Orthodox Monastery of St. George of Choziba.

We descended from the coach in an isolated spot on this high, concave stretch of white sandy wilderness with its canopy of blue sky overhead. It was by now late afternoon and the sun was low in the west. We followed Michael to a look-out point where he pointed down to the shadowed canyon far below.

"Can you see the blue dome and buildings built against the rock?" he asked.

It was astonishing. Way below, tucked against the layered strata of rock, clung the huddled buildings of this monastery with its blue domed bell-tower.

"By golly! how does anybody get to it?" enquired the W.I. woman.

"There is a footpath along the Wadi," Michael said. "It first became a monastery in the fifth century. Before that there were Christian hermits living in caves who gathered there for liturgies and communal worship."

The Scottish minister told us how the road down in the gorge was the site of Jesus' parable about the Good Samaritan.

Its desolation and absolute isolation was made for brigands. I wondered what I'd do if I came across some beaten-up fellow – probably run. The Scottish minister told us how the Samaritans at the time of Jesus had been looked down on by the Judaeans because they were of mixed race and not truly Jewish. "And for your information," said the Scottish minister, "there is down there the Inn of the Good Samaritan."

"Will we be going there?" enquired the Irish girl.

"Sadly, no. It's already late," he remarked, looking at his watch.

Word must have got around that a tourist bus had arrived, because out of nowhere Arab children appeared beside us as if by magic, holding up trinkets and worthless small objects to sell. Their pleading brown eyes and ragged clothes prompted me to buy a bead necklace I really didn't want. This encouraged the rest of the rabble to clamour around till I myself began to feel in need of a Good Samaritan to keep these small would-be robbers off my back.

★

In my notebook that night I wrote: *Really wish we could go to see the Monastery of St. George of Choziba. The guide-book says that legend has it Elijah stayed in a cave there when he was fleeing from Jezebel and was on his way to Sinai. Also the father of the Virgin Mary, Joachim, was there – where? In a cave? And was informed by an angel that his daughter had had an immaculate conception. Wonder what he was doing there on the side of the canyon? Very odd. People love weird, imaginative stories.*

I must write about the Dead Sea. After Masada we had lunch beside the Dead Sea and afterwards bathed in it which felt strange. Hate swimming but thought I must take a dip with the others. Very difficult to get your feet back down to the sea-bed when floating. Took a photo of some woman lying on the water and reading a book.

Tomorrow the Canon is taking some of us to Bethlehem to meet a friend of his, a Palestinian Christian. Am really looking forward to that, especially as in the evening we've been invited to his nephew's engagement party. Interesting!

A PALESTINIAN CHRISTIAN'S HOME

CHAPTER

5

BETHLEHEM
AGAIN

We took an Arab bus from the bus station just around from our hotel. I found myself seated beside the Canon who told me a little about the Palestinian Christian who lived in Bethlehem, to whose house we were going. The Canon had known him for some years and told me that X was not a man afraid to speak his mind about the problems he and his family faced under Israeli occupation.

"On these tours I think it important to get into a Palestinian home and hear about their difficulties," he said.

I loved the fact we were on a local bus and not going on our coach. Several Arab women were on board and there were a few rough looking men in *keffiyehs*. We got out at Bet Jala, a Palestinian village, where we were met by three taxis sent by X to bring us into Bethlehem. I wondered why we were going this way and not through the checkpoint we'd passed through on our initial visit.

These various entries to Bethlehem reminded me of a book I'd read by a Palestinian Lutheran priest living in Bethlehem. He'd experienced a harrowing ordeal when his father-in-law had been taken ill one night. Because the hospital in Bethlehem had been unable to treat him satisfactorily the family had decided to get him to a hospital in Jerusalem. He'd been taken by ambulance to the Israeli check-point (I supposed the one we'd come through on our first visit). He had all the appropriate documents giving him permission to travel to Jerusalem, but the soldier on duty had been in a bad mood and had refused to allow him through. The soldier claimed that the priest's father-in-law was not going to Jerusalem on business as stated on his permit and, therefore, couldn't be allowed to pass. After much argument the family had been compelled to try another route, maybe the one here at Bet Jala? But the soldier on duty at that check-point had said that, although the patient's documents were in order, the ambulance itself wouldn't be allowed to pass. The family finally had had to phone for an ambulance to come out from Jerusalem to pick up the invalid. This unnecessary delay had proved fatal and the priest's father-in-law had died.

After reading this story I had felt incredulous that the Christian Palestinian Lutheran priest still believed that by prayer and faith in God their problems would be overcome. God would save them was his certain belief.

I confided my thoughts to the Canon as I sat beside him on the bus. He acknowledged that prayer alone might seem trivial but, when all else failed, the only thing that remained was prayer. "Violence hasn't helped the Palestinians, they've tried that and have suffered severe reprisals as a consequence," he said.

"But supposing in World War II we'd merely knelt down and prayed that Germany would lose the war?" I demanded.

"I take your point. But here it's too late. The Israelis have the authority and the backing of the U.S." I knew he was in sympathy with the Palestinians. "I'm glad you're getting the opportunity to meet X," he continued calmly. "You'll find him very easy to talk to. He welcomes questions, and you can ask him anything you want."

★

I'd been expecting a poverty stricken Arab and was surprised when we were put down before a large house, on the ground floor of which was his shop. The shop was fairly non-descript containing glass display cabinets in which were plates of biscuits and a few cakes. We were shown to the back of the shop where there were three or four small tables and plastic chairs.

X was an imposing man with a good Arab nose, thick dark moustache, a balding head and alert, intelligent brown eyes. He had charisma and an air of authority.

"Welcome, welcome! Welcome to Bethlehem!" He had an expansive stomach, and was dressed in an open-necked white shirt and dark trousers held up by a plaited leather belt. We were all at first slightly inhibited by the occasion, but he was eager to put us at our ease and asked us what we would like to drink. I felt we should ask for water (but maybe water was a problem). The others were less cautious and asked for apple juice, Coca-Cola and suchlike.

We were then introduced collectively to his wife who stood by a stove cooking a large chicken dish for her twelve guests. She was a tall, well-built beauty with shoulder-length dark hair and lively humorous eyes. She wore European clothes and had on an apron. B (this is what I will call her) smiled cheerfully as she stirred the casserole in a large roasting tin.

Twelve guests to lunch? No problem! X didn't offer to help his wife, it's not the Arab way. Any help came from unseen female helpers. Instead, he sat on a chair and began to talk. He wasn't afraid to speak his mind openly, never mind the consequences, they would be dealt with later if necessary.

He began by talking about his family. He had seven children, aged from their mid-twenties downwards, his youngest being a twelve year old girl. I immediately thought of the expense of feeding and clothing them and the cost of house repairs. "Please ask me any questions you like," he invited. He was a very confident figure seated in his chair, his bright, inquisitive eyes assessing us all continuously.

The Canon enquired about the engagement party to which we were all invited that evening. How many guests would there be? Five hundred, said X without batting an eyelid. Five hundred? And a thousand at the wedding itself, he added. Had he said this to impress us? He appeared nonchalant, very happy to let us glean that there was obviously money in the family. With money comes influence and authority. In fact we were to learn that one of his relations was standing in the next local elections as a Fatah candidate and hoped to become mayor of Bethlehem. I had supposed that all Palestinians lived in poverty and struggled to scrape a living.

X went on to speak about another property he owned near to Bethlehem and an apartment he had in Jerusalem. But, he was quick to add, he lacked the one essential ingredient to a happy life and that was freedom. He could do nothing without first getting Israeli permission. Because of the Israeli occupation everything had to be referred to the authorities – the Israeli authorities.

Bethlehem was a town under twenty-four hour curfew, he said, which I supposed meant they were not allowed out of Bethlehem without papers permitting them to travel to some stated destination.

He began to expand at length on the restrictions. For example, in order to get the best education for his children which could only be had in Jerusalem, it was necessary for his wife to live there.

"My wife has a blue Jerusalem I.D. card and I have a green Palestinian I.D. and a Palestinian passport. But my wife cannot have a Palestinian passport or she will lose her Jerusalem I.D. card. With my Palestinian I.D. I can go anywhere I like but only with Israeli authorization," he said. "What I am telling you is that my wife can only come to Bethlehem these few miles away once a week or she will lose her Jerusalem I.D. card. Equally, if I go to Jerusalem and stay with my wife I will be arrested. If she has come here for her one day permit and I drive her back to Jerusalem without Israeli authorization then her car will be confiscated, her licence taken away and she will be fined." He shook his head sadly. "Can you imagine what sort of a life we have? My wife cannot be with me except for one day a week."

We looked at him and commiserated; it was all we could do. He went on to tell us how his wife's parents were in ill health but he was refused a permit to travel to see them. When his son had had surgery in Jerusalem he hadn't been allowed to visit him either.

There were many spies in Bethlehem and he had his mobile phone regularly checked, he said. The Israeli Civil Intelligence Authority was all powerful and all final decisions were taken by it. It was clear, he added, that the Israelis were hoping to drive the Palestinians out of Bethlehem altogether.

"Let me tell you," he went on. "I have an American

friend from Wisconsin who wanted to visit me here in Bethlehem. He was travelling with a group and had an Israeli tour guide. But his tour guide warned him that if he came to see me the Israeli security police at the airport would be informed and he would have difficulty in getting out of Israel. This is the situation here. The Israelis are in control. I waited all day for my friend to come but he was warned not to, and he never telephoned me."

The Irish girl asked: "What about the Palestinian government?"

X was prompt with his reply: "The Palestinian government is a government only in name and has no power." He began to shift the subject slightly from the problems with the Israelis to further problems existing between the Palestinian Moslems and Christians.

"Let me tell you there are now only six to eight thousand Christians left here in Bethlehem, half a million of us have now gone to live abroad. To open a business in the town it is easier to say you are a Moslem, even if in your heart you are a Christian."

It was curious detecting these wheels within wheels of conflict. Not only were they suffering under the Israelis, but suffering due to Christian and Moslem differences and jealousies. It seemed an unending conflict caused entirely by religion.

"Have you ever considered leaving?" I asked X.

He eyed me with his lively inquisitive look. "Where would we go?" he enquired. "No, we will never leave. My family has lived here for centuries. My family, you must understand, came originally from the Yemen. They were there before Islam came to the Yemen. To tell you the truth we are Arab Yemenis and one of the first Christians." X was in full spate. he was extremely articulate and his English was fluent. "But you ask me if I would leave Bethlehem and the answer is no. I believe it is better for us to stay and face the dangers we know here, than to go to a foreign country where we must face the dangers we do not know." And he spoke extensively about the problems he had read that existed on the streets of London and America. He had a point. "You can only die once and I would prefer to die in my own country," he said.

His wife declared that lunch was ready and we were asked to come and help ourselves from a serving table. Harry, who was always suspicious of foreign dishes, took a diminutive helping until B insisted she pile up his plate with rice, salad and more chicken casserole.

"Ummmm. Hummm. Well, thank you!"

"We cannot send you home hungry from your visit here in our house," she remarked.

"No. Yes. Well – thank you!"

"Can I give you more of the sauce? Look! it is good!" and she dipped a finger in it and licked it with her beautiful lips. "Take a little. Please, try it!" And she offered him a teaspoon of it. Harry obediently sampled it and agreed that it was excellent and more sauce was added.

He joined me at the table with a loaded plate of what he saw as a pile of lethal germs. I was the one with a small helping but only because I felt they needed as much left-overs as possible for the family to eat the following day. To have twelve well fed westerners gobbling Palestinian food seemed somehow wrong and inexcusable.

The W.I. woman was interested in the dish before her. What was the recipe? Could she write down the ingredients? Was it exclusively Palestinian? Could she detect a little paprika? A little coriander? Ah, ginger! – Cooked with olive oil? Good? Wasn't it just!

B was delighted with this praise and interest which, no doubt, would be passed on to the Women's Institute in England. What better accolade than that from those singers of 'Jerusalem'!

After the meal their daughter-in-law arrived with a hairdresser friend of hers, and they disappeared through the shop to another room amidst much female jollity. As B herself was going to have her hair done for the party that evening, she left us and we were taken upstairs to a large sitting-room where there were several sofas, armchairs and a large television in a corner.

X sat himself comfortably and continued to expound on the difficulties he had to face daily.

"For instance," he began, "I am part of a co-operative owning an olive grove from which are made olive wood trinkets and ornaments." He passed his hand over his brow and jaw in a despairing gesture. "But now our olive trees are on the wrong side of the Israeli wall so the people of Bethlehem cannot harvest the olives or get the wood without Israeli permission."

He went on to say how he used to travel to America in order to sell his olive wood objects but now it was no longer viable. You could see by his lively, energetic face that he was not one to be easily defeated and he went on: "But I have other plans. I am thinking of turning some of our rooms into apartments for tourists coming to Bethlehem. I hope also to have a restaurant up on the top floor of our house. Would you like to come and see?"

"Oh, yes, I would," said the Irish girl.

"Did you say a restaurant?" asked the W.I. woman. "Oh, I don't want to miss that!"

I was also on my feet. Harry was settled firmly in his armchair, and the Canon who had heard X relating his problems before, declined. The others also wanted to relax.

X led the way. As we passed an open door we caught sight of B having her hair washed by her daugter-in-law's friend. Her head was back over a smart looking wash-hand-basin in what, at a glance, appeared to be an otherwise empty room. The corridor and stairways had no carpets or furniture and we stepped over loops of cabling spread along the concrete floor.

We came out on to the flat roof where steel spikes were in place to build a new storey for what he hoped would be his restaurant.

"It will be the best restaurant in Bethlehem," declared X with pride. "It will be all glass so that the diners can see Bethlehem all around."

"So what sort of food are you planning for your menus?" asked the W.I. woman with interest.

X was somewhat evasive and thought his wife would know the answer to that.

"Well, if it's anything like luncheon today, by golly!" and she put on a sort of gastronomic appreciation act.

"I like it here," said the Irish girl. "Do you have to get Israeli permission to build?"

"Of course!" X eyed her. "We all have to have dreams," he said. He turned and pointed to some distant houses built up the side of a hill. "That is an Israeli settlement. We have many of them around Bethlehem." And he went on to tell us how the Israelis had plans to build luxury hotels in their settlements which would undoubtedly take the tourist trade away from the Palestinians. The pilgrims would visit the holy sites by day but would then return to the Israeli hotels afterwards for their five star treatment and evening entertainment. He shrugged. "What can we do? We can do nothing without Israeli authorization. But to convert our rooms to pilgrim apartments is my dream. I have to try."

The W.I. woman smiled and hugged herself comfortably but said nothing. She had a lively expression but knew when it was better to keep silent. I suspected she supported the Jews.

The sight of the Israeli settlements overlooking Bethlehem I thought sinister. There was a feeling of always being watched by those who wanted you gone; of your enemy looking through powerful binoculars and awaiting the moment he sees you pack your bags in order to move in and seize your coveted land and property.

Israelis, X went on, were very, very clever at putting out propaganda which put the Palestinians in the wrong whilst the Israelis were seen as the poor victims. Whenever there was violence from the Palestinians, then the Israelis would take immediate reprisal measures with their superior weapons and American financial backing, claiming to be acting in self-defence and accusing the Palestinians of being the aggressors.

We came down from the roof and passed two of his children playing pool at a table in an otherwise unfurnished room. X excused himself for a moment and returned with some of his olive wood ornaments and wooden bead necklaces with crosses hanging from them. He said he just wanted us to see the sort of things his co-operative made.

"Are they for sale?" we asked.

He put on an act of not having brought them to us to sell, but we all knew he could do with the money if we did buy them.

"How much are they?" we enquired.

"Nothing. It is a gift." X shrugged.

"No, you must tell us how much!" we insisted.

He shrugged some more and said it was up to us, he would like us to take our pick. They were nothing, we could have them as a gift.

We all bought, and I ignored Harry's hissing whisper that I would never wear one. "Maybe not," I agreed, but I can give it as a Christmas present – from Bethlehem and all that. In fact I'll buy two."

Harry knew better than to hiss any more or I might buy three.

The W.I. woman bought six, declaring her intense interest in local craftmanship – olive wood – hand worked – was it difficult to bore holes in the beads? – was it just! – presents from Bethlehem for all her numerous friends – yes – can't get better value than that!"

One of X's sons appeared and sat down with as much confidence as his father. He had been for a while in America at university having applied successfully for a grant. But he had only stayed six months because the grant had been stopped.

He was incredibly religious and said he was a Melkite Christian. What on earth was that? I didn't like to ask but later found out that the Melkites originated in the eleventh century when the king of Constantinople (in other words the emperor) sided with the Pope against the Greek Orthodox Patriarch of Constantinople. The 'Melk' part of the word comes from *'malik'* meaning 'king' in Arabic. The Melkites are also called Greek Catholics but have the same liturgies and traditions as the Greek Orthodox Church.

This son had great faith and declared that if you wanted to do something then you should never be afraid to attempt it, so long as you knew it was good and right. He believed in the holy writ of the Bible and declared roundly that in the West there was far too much emphasis on the freedom of the body and not enough concentration on freedom of the soul. In the West, he announced, they believed more in money than in God.

He seemed to be a confident younger version of his father and very eloquent in his outpourings. It was almost as though he had learned it all by heart. He had been in America during 9/11.

"What had that been like for him?" I asked.

"It was all right for me," he replied, "because I was a Christian and was living in a Christian community with a Christian family. But I know others who were not so fortunate, and they had a very difficult time." He went on to tell us that at university one of his friends had been killed (he didn't elaborate on how or where), and afterwards he hadn't been able to concentrate on his studies, so he had come home. I had wanted to ask if that was why his grant had been stopped but had thought it more prudent to stay silent.

X returned and spoke at large to the others about his restaurant ambitions and the likelihood of having his request for a permit rejected by the Israelis.

"You have to stand up and fight!" I found myself saying.

Father and son eyed me and the son said firmly that he put his faith in God. I felt myself pumping up with indignation at this apparent pacifism which so blatantly played into the hands of the Israelis. I noticed also the W.I. woman's lively eyes watching and waiting for a collision of minds into which she herself might jump in with her own Zionist views.

X saw my militancy and began to speak about fellow Palestinians some of whom, he said, were bad people because they carried guns. I immediately wanted to ask if they couldn't be described as freedom fighters. I wanted to shout out in my frustration that they couldn't just pray for God's assistance because he clearly wasn't helping – wasn't there, didn't exist even.

But again I remained silent. How could I know anything of their problems when I had only been there a few hours? They had to have their dreams even if it was only that the Almighty would help. Anyway, for all I knew the room was bugged and all conversation was being recorded. I wondered if X knew it was and wanted us to be overheard by the Israeli authorities who mightn't like their brutal tactics to be the subject of discussion with westerners. I wondered if I might be arrested at the airport for suggesting they stand up and fight. Maybe, maybe –

Conversation shifted to the subject of marriage. X's own marriage had been an arranged one, he said. That was interesting. In this they resembled the ultra-Orthodox Jews I'd met on the plane. Families decided on the suitability of a respective son- or daughter-in-law, and all would be arranged by the parents, we were told. A meeting of the son and daughter would be fixed, and then the engagement would be announced and there would be a month's engagement before the marriage.

"It is the best way," said X, in full spate again. "You have only to look to the more liberated countries to see that seventy to eighty percent of love marriages end in divorce. Here in our society the majority know only one man or one woman and only when they are married." And he went on to expound how divorce was unusual in his community because of family ties, and the pressure put on couples to stay together.

At this point B came in with her hair newly washed and set, waved and highlighted. She was stunningly beautiful and quite unselfconscious.

We were invited to go and get ourselves ready for the evening party. Some of the women among us had brought a change of clothing, though most had brought accessories to spruce themselves up.

Beyond the sitting-room was the master bedroom and a bathroom. This part of the house was clearly the most furnished and lived in. The family now was in a flurry of activity as they got themselves washed and changed for the evening celebrations. I left Harry and went and dolled myself up for the occasion which meant putting on a bit of lipstick and eyeshadow. B came into the bedroom looking a million dollars and appearing totally relaxed as though the occasion was a daily event. I wished I had brought something better to change into to meet the standards of this Palestinian family, but it was too late to worry. The rest of the family appeared and the youngest daughter, not yet a teenager, had her dark glossy hair drawn back into cascading curls. She too one day would be a beauty.

"Are you all right there in the back?" B called, glancing at us in her rear mirror with her lively, beautifully made-up eyes.

We'd been hurled to the left, then to the right, whiplashed forwards as she screeched to a halt to avoid oncoming vehicles, and whiplashed backwards as she accelerated for more overtakings.

"Yes, we're fine!" I said as we hurtled along the straight for a while.

"Ask her where we're going," Harry muttered.

"We're going to the Bethlehem Hotel," said B, glancing at him over her shoulder. "It's not long now."

Her tyres smoked as she braked to a halt before backing

swiftly and expertly into a wall – well, within an inch of it. "We've arrived!" she said triumphantly. She got out of the car (a very old bone-shaker and one day, no doubt, a bone breaker), smoothed down her sylph-like garments, and switched from being the demon driver to the glamorous beauty queen again.

Soon we were shaking hands with the engaged couple's parents at the Bethlehem Hotel, and being shepherded across a large banqueting hall to a table in a far corner. It occurred to me that maybe X's relation wasn't too pleased to have a dozen more British citizens added to his already numerous guests. His greeting of us had been cordial but not enthusiastic.

An oval table draped in a white cloth had a three-tiered cake centrally placed on it. Expensive floral decorations spiralled up pillars in the hall.

The engaged couple appeared, the intended bride in an expensive looking patterned chiffon dress, her black, glossy hair carefully arranged in sweeps and swirls at the nape of her neck. Like B she was very glamorous. Her fiancé wore a dark suit, white shirt and tie. He must have been in his late twenties and I was told that he was studying Medicine up at Cambridge. There was not only money but brains in the family.

A long table to one side of the room had priests sitting at it. When all the guests were gathered and the parents had taken their seats, we were all asked to stand and one of the priests started to chant prayers with 'Ameen' (Amen) at the end of each. His black garments and headgear were unlike any I had seen before and I supposed he was a Melkite. After the prayers he approached the young couple and placed a garland around the neck of the bride-to-be.

Amplified music started and the dancing began with the engaged couple taking to the floor – well, not exactly because both were raised up on chairs – not the easiest way to dance. In due course they were both lowered to the ground and were able to dance in a rather more normal fashion. The music was mostly Arab interspersed with English pop. Dancing consisted of jiving energetically before your partner, or on your own. It was all very lively and B took to the floor at once with her young daughter.

After five minutes during which we all sat with X and the rest of his family watching (X said firmly he never danced and couldn't dance), B came down between the tables and waved to us to join her.

Harry was adamant that he was not going to make an exhibition of himself among these foreigners – foreigners? – well, all right, he was the foreigner – whatever anybody was he wasn't going to dance, so there.

I was bewitched by the Arab music and the rhythm, and followed B's lead which consisted of sinuous movements of the arms and body, then thrusting out a hip to the beat, whilst doing random twisting movements with the feet.

There was a couple of very attractive young Moslem girls, their faces with their olive complexions beautifully made up with eye shadow and a light dusting of rouge. Their heads were covered by the white Moslem head scarf, and their long clothing looked elegant. They were happily dancing together when suddenly the elder seized my hand and drew me towards her to dance.

It was impossible to speak or be heard above the music. When later I went to the cloak-room I was followed by these two Moslem girls. I'd taken them for teenagers, but was now told by the elder of them that she was thirty-two and was the aunt of the other who was twenty-three.

The aunt asked for my telephone number in case she ever came to England. She was a teacher but was hoping to do a PhD in environmental studies. Wasn't she married, I asked inquisitively? She replied that she was too ambitious and preferred to be on her own. She earned her living by teaching science and maths.

I went back to our table and found Harry eating a chocolate, a bowlful of which had been passed around. We all had water or Coca-Cola to drink. He looked gloomily at his glass and wanted to know whether we'd be staying all night. I tried to persuade him to come and dance as it would pass the time, but he thought that sounded worse than sitting and sipping water.

Soon the music ended and the young couple cut the cake with a sword and the W.I. woman played at 'guessing the ingredients of the cake' which looked to me like an ordinary sponge. The music started up again with Cliff Richard's once top-of-the-charts 'Congratulations... and celebrations...' We were all given a piece of cake and I ignored the W.I. woman's queries as to how long and at what temperature it had been baked – or what sort of jam in the filling?

We drank the health of the newly engaged couple with a dash of champagne. After this they began a slow smooching dance together. I wondered if theirs had been an arranged marriage and, if so, had they known each other earlier? The couple looked as though they were in love.

Again B waved us over to the dancing and once more I joined her. The Irish girl was still gyrating in a totally unaware-of-anyone-else sort of way. Her movements were erratic and jerky with no sense of rhythm at all.

After a while I walked over to our table and positively insisted that X should come out to join us. I said I wouldn't take no for an answer and it didn't matter if he couldn't dance as neither could I. To my surprise he got up and followed me. On the dance floor he began to dance with abandon. His expression was one of resigned pleasure, and in no time I found myself being whirled under his extended arm. This was fun!

After about five minutes, I began to think that any more whirling and I'd fall flat on my face, so I firmly handed him across to B. As husband and wife they might as well make the most of their few hours permitted together.

As I came back to our table I passed an effete young man in jeans with blond hair; he seemed rather bemused and quite out of place.

"Are you from around here?" I asked when I was beside him.

He told me he was Irish, or at least had Irish ancestry though he was, in fact American. Since the Iraqi war it was easier to say he was from Ireland while working with the Palestinians.

"Irish!" I said. "Then you must meet the young Irish girl in our party!"

His eyes lit up at the thought and he came and sat at our table. Meanwhile the Irish girl continued dancing in her jerky, unrhythmic manner, her eyes more closed than open, her curly hair framing a face that was flushed and perspiring.

I learned from the young man that he was doing drama therapy with an organization called Project Hope, and that he worked with Palestinians, helping them to overcome their numerous traumatic experiences. He explained how he taught them to act out their deepest psychological problems as victims of war.

I wished I was in a position to see him do this. I took

down the details of his work and was given a website where I could learn more about the project.

The Irish girl returned to the table looking rather wild. I introduced her to the Irishman and she began to dart quick and demure glances at him. I was pleased to see they were getting along well. Perhaps he would be a new man in her life? Five minutes later, however, all was over between them. The Irishman excused himself and was soon gone.

"Pity," I said to the Irish girl, when he had departed. "I really thought you might hit it off."

"You didn't? With him?"

"Well – " I gestured that it was the best I could do.

"He's a pansy!"

I had to admit I'd thought so too but I'd thought it worth a try. Anyway it had been interesting hearing about his drama therapy and how it helped individuals who'd had their homes bombed or bull-dozed, or who'd lost relatives.

The party broke up at about ten o'clock. I noticed the W.I. woman having difficulty in staying awake as were most of her companions.

Back out in the street we had to spend some time for our transport to be organized to take us back to Jerusalem. While we waited I leaned on a parapet wall and surveyed Bethlehem by night. Its comparative silence belied the true facts. X had warned us when we'd been at his house, not to be alarmed if we heard shooting. It would be nothing serious, but there were certain ongoing private vendettas which occasionally flared up, he'd said.

At no time whilst in Bethlehem, however, had we really been aware of the underlying violence that existed there beneath the surface. It was odd how secure we felt in a town in torment.

★

That night I wrote in my notes: *Fascinating day! But to do nothing more than pray? To believe that by prayer your situation will change for the better? Things can really only change by human action bringing about the changes needed – they only change if the stronger recognizes the needs of the weaker and believes in justice.*

Tomorrow is Pentecost and am expecting the Holy Spirit to descend in tongues of fire. I may have doubts about God, but feel there might be a spirit. Define spirit? Can't. Too late to think anymore.

Anyway, tomorrow will be interesting.

CHAPTER

6

JERUSALEM
AND BETHANY

The congregation was ecstatic, many of them had their faces turned heavenwards, eyes shut, arms raised in the air with the palms of their hands turned upwards. In the previous hymn they had been dancing in the pews and letting out shrieks and yells of delirium.

The church we were in was Charismatic, Ecumenical, Protestant – in fact, appealing to all sects. The priest was praying about the need for the Church to take the lead in peace – love – forgiveness – understanding – reconciliation – all the things which sounded good from a priest but which often withered in the bud when put to the test.

On the altar, alongside a chalice and cross, was a menorah (seven-branched candlestick) to remind the congregation that Christianity had its roots in Judaism. It was an attempt to stretch out a Christian hand of goodwill to the Jews. It was all very well meaning and noble but the reality, despite all the Church prayers and sermons from pulpits, fell far short of achieving peace among men.

The menorah of the first temple had always been kept burning – it was symbolic of the eternal light of God.

Today the menorah is the emblem of the modern state of Israel.

Apparently, the first original menorah had appeared when Moses had thrown a lump of gold onto a fire and it had miraculously self-created itself. It had been housed in Solomon's temple and had been kept burning (like the eternal flame at Olympia and other ancient Greek temples) fuelled by pure, sanctified olive oil – a goddess Athena idea?

Before coming on this trip I'd read books by the great pioneers who'd set out to make their dreams of Zionism a reality – Ben Gurion, Menachem Begin, Moshe Dayan, Golda Meir and others. They had all been born into poverty in Eastern Europe, and their families had lived in constant fear of persecution. When still in their teens these young pioneers had been driven by a vision of a Zionist state and a return to the homeland of their forefathers.

Forging the new State of Israel had been an almost insurmountable task, yet it had been done with amazing courage, fortitude, and daring. To create a democracy and the Knesset; to found universities, hospitals, and vital institutions; to train the armed forces to a degree capable of defending the newly created country against overwhelming odds; to keep up morale and convince the world of their rights to the land and their good intentions; to make Hebrew the common language so Jews from all parts of the world, speaking a multitude of tongues, could communicate with each other – all these problems had somehow to be surmounted. That it had all finally come together seemed as if a divine hand really had been at work inspiring these exceptionally bold characters with formidable enthusiasm and determination to establish their new State of Israel.

But it had left out the needs of the Palestinians.

Ben Gurion had been the first prime minister of Israel. I'd been surprised and shocked when I'd read that his vision for Israel had been for a secular State; that he didn't believe that the Bible was divinely inspired. His views were that the basis of Jewish religion was its association with the land of Israel; he didn't agree with the ultra-Orthodox Jews (though he respected their beliefs) that every Jew should practise his religion, observe the Sabbath and attend synagogue. I found it very odd that there should be a State of Israel for Jews if religion wasn't the main factor for it. Why bother to go to all the pain and trouble to reclaim the Jewish homeland if their religion which first bound Jews together was no longer the main factor?

At the birth of the new State of Israel Ben Gurion read out a declaration in which he promised liberty, justice, and peace, social and political equality without regard to race, sex, or religion. He also declared that Israel would co-operate with the United Nations. Israel, he said, held out the hand of peace to Arabs everywhere. All wonderfully inspiring words but, like the words of the vicar preaching love and forgiveness, they were soon forgotten when faced with the reality on the ground; in the face of strong Palestinian opposition his words proved to be no more than a string of false promises.

To get back to the menorah. On one of the days in Jerusalem, Michael took us to the Cardo in the Jewish Quarter of the city, where he pointed out a very large and solid gold menorah exhibited in a centrally placed reinforced glass cabinet for all to see. It was there awaiting the day when it could be placed in the Holy of Holies in a newly built temple. That meant destroying the Dome of the Rock. There was no secrecy about it, no subtlety, just a heart-on-sleeve long held Jewish ambition; an agony-in-waiting for the Moslems, or else for the Jews, if things went the wrong way for them.

The vicar's sermon at this Pentecostal service seemed never ending. His voice had crescendoed from hushed confidential appeals to positively yelling that we were to allow the Holy Spirit into our hearts. His bellowing set a toddler in a playpen screaming with terror.

The young mother who had been playing a violin had to atted to the little mite. The priest appeared not to notice the child's uproar, he himself was too possessed.

His voice bellowed and echoed around the church, telling us how God was trying to wake us all up. Was he, by gum! A woman on the other side of the aisle occasionally shouted 'Alleluyia!'

I had come to this Pentecostal service optimistically expecting the heavens to open or, at the very least, to receive some help from the Holy Spirit to give me a glimmer of understanding of what it was all about, but I was growing increasingly exasperated.

It was a merciful release when the sermon finally ended and the congregation, accompanied by the mother on her violin (she had managed to silence her child), sang a hymn:

'God of Elijah, hear our cry, send the fire!
And make us fit to live or die and send the fire today.
To burn up every trace of sin,
To bring the light and glory in,
The revolution now begin!
Send the fire today!
Send the fire today!

Spirit of the living God
Fall afresh on me.

Spirit of the living God
Fall afresh on me.
Break me, melt me,
Mould me, fill me...'

These words were accompanied by increasing wailings and warblings, clapping of hands and stamping of feet. Looking around I was astonished how people could become so demented in their cravings for whatever they were craving.

This was a Holy Communion service and I knew I didn't want to take the Sacraments here, but neither did I want to offend the Canon or anyone else in our group. I was aware of a strange fluttering around my rib cage and wondered if this could possibly be the Holy Spirit trying to enter. After a few seconds I realized that it was, in fact, nothing more than intense irritation.

The usual prayers of penitence and the accusation that we were miserable sinners were said. "Why?" I'd once found myself demanding of the vicar at home, when I'd been at a Bible study session of the Acts of the Apostles and had been surrounded by confirmed Church goers, "why is there so much emphasis on sin in Christianity?" I hadn't been admonished but had been made to feel I'd made a valid point, which was kind of the vicar. He pointed out that God was so holy that we always fell far short of being able to attain to his perfection.

"Yes, I can see that," I'd said, slightly abashed at the fact that I'd blurted out the 'Why?' in the first place. "But surely we all do our best in our own way and don't have to keep repenting about not having done better?" Someone else had said, "I know I'm a miserable sinner. I'm very aware of it all the time."

"But you're not a miserable sinner," I'd objected. "You do what you can to help others; you don't go around stealing or murdering. Anyway, to do good deeds constantly would be to drown yourself in goodness and to lose your real identity. And besides, the more you do the less other people do, so you are in fact making other people into sinners whilst overloading yourself with piety which is a sort of sin in itself. Certainly if I was too full of piety and goodness it would drive Harry mad. There has to be a balance!"

The vicar had been kind, conciliatory and the reading of Acts had continued, but not before I'd enquired why the early Church Fathers, or whoever had been responsible for early Church liturgy, had concentrated so much on sin when they could as easily have established a liturgy where the congregation could place before God the good things they'd done. It must be very depressing for poor God to be loaded only with men's sins every week into eternity, I'd remarked.

The time for Communion was upon us and I received the prod I'd expected from Harry. I stepped out into the aisle and stood my ground, allowing the others to come out of the pew. I didn't repent and I wasn't going up, so went back in the pew and knelt down with my head in my hands so Harry could neither prod nor pull.

Peace? Love? There had never been peace and precious little love when it had come to Christian sectarian bickerings, anti-Semitism, Crusader wars, inquisitions, religious intolerance.

I'd once tackled a kindly priest, I'd just happened to be sitting beside at some wedding reception, when he'd said rather pompously that the greatest of all things was love as St. Paul had said. "What do you mean by love?" I'd suddenly asked. "The word has so many meanings! There are so many different facets to it. You can fall in love, or love cooking, or love the summer. What do you mean by the word 'love'?" Hum. Haw. Hum. He threw the question back at me: "What would you say is the most important thing in life?" he asked. "Duty," I'd replied, surprising myself as much as I'd surprised him. "If everybody stopped wallowing in this word 'love' and, instead, did what they knew was their duty, wouldn't the world be better?"

On reflection, I supposed 'love' was something you couldn't discipline into yourself. You either loved or felt you ought to love, and you knew whether you did or didn't or should. Duty was different. Duty was a discipline that had to be practised for the benefit of society as a whole.

Now in the heart of Jerusalem on the day of Pentecost I came out of the church triumphant because I had rebelled at last and had remained in the pew and not taken the sacraments. I hadn't pretended to a love I didn't feel, or performed a duty either, come to that.

"There was no need for you to refuse to take communion," Harry said afterwards. "There was no harm in going up and conforming."

"I couldn't go up as an unrepentant sinner," I said.

"Of course you could!" came the prompt reply.

"I wanted to observe," I said firmly.

"You were just drawing attention to yourself," said the authority.

"I was very quiet about it," I said. "I wasn't shouting 'Alleluyia'. They were really drawing attention to themselves."

"You know what I mean," came Harry's reply.

"So, I suppose, you truly repented of all your sins, and really believed in what you were doing?"

"Of course!"

"Of course?"

"Yes. No. Yes. Well."

We had come to signs announcing Gents and Ladies, each pointing in opposite directions, and our ways parted.

It was pitch black in the Ladies. "Can you find the switch?" asked the Canon's wife kindly. I searched around in the dark aware that I was following the line of some rather suspect wiring. If I was electrocuted then, no doubt, it would be divine retribution, and I braced myself for the shock, uncertain if I could face being brought before the Almighty in my present mood of defiance.

I pressed the switch. The light came on in our darkness and the Canon's wife said "Oh, well done!" and I remained alive and well.

It was the afternoon and we were driving through Bethany. There was everywhere a general air of hopelessness and despair with refuse and scrap-iron piled up by the roadside. Bethany is in the West Bank. At the time of Christ it was a small village where Martha, Mary and Lazarus (friends of Jesus) lived. It was where Lazarus had died and Jesus had miraculously brought him back to life.

We were taken to see the tomb from which Lazarus was raised. "Mind your step, please!" Michael shouted, remaining above ground as we took turns descending the stone steps to the tomb. "Hold on to the rail, please!"

I supposed it was all very interesting. I had seen his tomb in Cyprus, a grandiose affair in Larnaca. One always thinks of Lazarus as having been raised from the dead, never as having finally died.

We were driven to the Jeel Al-Amal Boys' Orphanage. It was a large cream-coloured building with a school yard.

We were invited in and taken to a large hall where five boys of different ages were singing Palestinian songs to welcome us; they were accompanied by one of the staff on an electric keyboard. They sang with gusto as we were shown to seats along one wall.

Soon small boys, aged between five and eight years old, marched in wearing bright yellow, red or green football shirts. They were ushered in by the house matron who made sure that they sat in an orderly group on the floor. Next came the older boys who sat around the room on chairs.

The last song had action to it and the boys stamped their feet, bent down to the ground and raised their arms up in the air. The Scottish minister told me afterwards he hadn't liked that song as he'd thought it 'subverrrsive'. But our coach driver who'd been in the hall and had translated the song for me later, declared that they were singing that the land was theirs, the earth was theirs and they were raising their arms to heaven calling for peace.

When the singing finished, the small figure of Alice Sahhar, a devout Christian and founder of the orphanage, entered with a fellow teacher who had lost an arm. She was an elderly woman full of confidence and determination. She exuded fearlessness and, after speaking for a while, it became clear she had an unbounding love for the children. We were told she was over seventy and was, in fact, very deaf.

Were there any questions we would like to put, we were asked? Yes, there were many. The man with her shouted our questions into her ear. How did she raise money to run her establishment?

By begging letters – through charities – by faith in God and by prayer, she replied promptly.

What about food? What about water for the hundred boys? They were all tidy and spotlessly clean in their football shirts.

Alice replied that they were blessed with their own well so today there was no problem. But there had been a time when there'd been no well and the orphanage had been under Israeli military curfew for many weeks, and at the time the water had been disconnected. Alice Sahhar could only pray, which was something she did every day, but had done even more so then. Quite unexpectedly, one day water had been detected seeping up under the dining-room floor, and a natural well had been discovered which Alice had known nothing about, even though she and her husband had bought the property years earlier.

On another occasion, without giving any reason, the Israelis had blockaded the entrance to the orphanage forcing anyone wanting to come or go to climb over huge boulders. Once there'd been so little food that the boys had had to survive on one potato a day. Alice had then learned from a baker friend in Jerusalem that he had plenty of bread but she would have to collect it. But the soldier at the Israeli check-point had refused to let her leave Bethany. There'd been only one way for her to get the food for the boys and she'd taken a great risk to herself and the orphanage. A van-driver had agreed to take her under cover of darkness by back roads out of Bethany to Jerusalem. There they'd loaded up the van with food and by good fortune had been able to return without detection.

As a Palestinian Christian herself did she only take Christian boys, I asked?

She took any child who was in need, she replied. Every child was God's creation. She had had some Christians, many more were Moslem and she'd even had some Jews.

She loved them all and would never turn a child away.

Alice Sahhar was convinced she was doing God's work, and as such was an optimist and full of hope for the future. But she'd had to overcome major crises in her life.

She'd been widowed and had now to struggle on alone. Some years back she'd fought off cancer declared by her doctors to be terminal. But she was a survivor and would never give in – not whilst any child needed her.

The small boys seated on the ground occasionally turned their heads to look at us. They were so young and vulnerable, I wanted to help them, I wanted to see them smile. I could understand Alice's dedication. She knew the tragedies and the traumas each had suffered. I was only an observer wanting to help for no more than an hour. If anyone was going to make me believe in the Almighty it was Alice Sahhar. Did I mean the Almighty? Or did I mean that power and energy which pervaded the world, something which human beings could tap into in times of dire stress.

I had brought out with me a bag of bright coloured tennis balls which I'd thought some Palestinian children might like, and I had them with me now hidden in a plastic bag. I didn't want any of the group to know I had them. At what seemed like a good moment I went over to the Moslem woman in charge of the small boys, and handed her the bag. She looked at me suspiciously, then peered into the bag and her eyes lit up at the sight of the balls, and she smiled and put a hand to my arm and whispered 'Shukran'.

One of the things that impressed me about the place was how the children were shown that life wasn't just about receiving from others but was about giving also. While we were there one of the youngest boys came in carrying a small canvas bag, and handed each one of us a bright blue paper dove with the word 'peace' on one side and 'shalom' on the other. A second boy followed him handing out from his canvas bag a brooch with a mother-of-pearl cross on it. Then later an older boy brought us all fruit juice.

We were shown over the school. Everywhere was spotless, the bedrooms neat and tidy. We were conducted to a terrace where we could look down over the playground where the boys were now kicking a football around with great enjoyment, small and older boys together in their football shirts playing at being David Beckhams.

I asked the man with one arm whether the boys went on to have careers? He looked at me as though I'd asked something really stupid. Of course, he answered. He himself had been one of the orphans there, and now had a doctorate. There were many from the orphanage who went on to get degrees. Those with less academic ability received training in some trade or skill. I wanted to ask him how he'd lost his arm, but I remained silent on the matter.

"We must give them something," I said to Harry who agreed, and we made a small contribution. Alice Sahhar didn't betray any sign of disappointment at the pittance. She was a woman who drew on all the resources available, and was schooled in being grateful for whatever came.

She told us how in a month's time she had seventeen Israeli women coming to the school which now had its own bakery. To have Israelis baking bread with Palestinian women was a symbol of hope. The E.U. was sending a delegation to witness this peaceful expression of unity. It was to celebrate the anniversary of the founding of her orphanage, she told us. I loved Alice Sahhar and her indomitable spirit. We eyed each other and, if ever I felt a surge of affection, it was for this woman in front of me.

I talked to an English woman who had come for two weeks as an assistant. In a few days, she told me, three more children were expected. Their Palestinian mother had been driven beyond endurance due to the pressures of life under Israeli occupation, and in her deranged state had murdered her husband. With their mother in gaol and their father dead what would become of the children?

Well, Alice Sahhar had the answer.

That night I wrote: *Alice Sahhar is the most amazing woman. A very strong character who looks forbidding but is so full of love you warm to her at once. Today I have seen two sides of Christianity, a demented 'Alleluyiah! Jesus lives!' one, and the opposite extreme of quiet, determined love-in-action one. Why do there have to be extremes? Socrates' theory of the law of contrasts?*

As for prayer! Well, I suppose I believe in the power of the mind which can bend events to its will if the will is strong enough. But the sudden appearance of a well? Did desperation make their search for water more thorough so they detected it where, in fact, it had always been? Might Alice Sahhar have recovered from cancer due to her mind and her own determination and drive?

My experiences today aren't going to make me pray, but they will prompt me to act/give/sponsor/do whatever I can to help where help is needed – i.e. give more money to the orphanage. Am I responding to Alice Sahhar's prayers, or quite simply to an obvious need?

Jesus said you must love your enemies. That hasn't come up in my Bible discussions yet. Not sure why one should love ones enemies really. Tolerate them, perhaps. Ignore them. Forgive them. But love them? Why would I even want to love them? I could try not to hate them, but I can't see the point of loving them. Forgive your brother 70 times 7, was another impossible bit of advice. A little correction on the part of the brother I would have thought wouldn't go amiss rather than endlessly forgiving him. Do ones duty by him, perhaps, but to keep forgiving only suggests that the brother is refusing to be reasonable. Seventy times seven is really giving that brother an unlimited opportunity to keep sinning. Not a good idea.

Tomorrow we go to Galilee. Although I'm looking forward to it, I don't want to leave Jerusalem for some strange and inexplicable reason.

CHAPTER

7

CAESAREA
AND TIBERIAS

As we drove north to Galilee we couldn't help noticing the intensive cultivation of the land. The Israelis had done what they claimed the Palestinians never bothered to do. Everywhere were prairie-like stretches of corn, acres of potato, and fields of vegetables. The sheer commitment to hard work was impressive.

Harry as a farmer was full of praise. "The Israelis have to be admired," he said. "Look at all that!"

"At the expense of the Palestinians," I added.

"The Palestinians never bothered – a grove of date palms, perhaps."

"They did as much as they needed to, and were happy," I said.

"Yes, but they didn't have the drive and purpose of the Israelis – all this proves it." And Harry waved a hand at the productive landscape.

"How would you feel if a farmer across the valley eyed your fields and because he saw docks and thistles decided to come across and plough it up to grow corn?" I demanded. "And if he said it was because you hadn't bothered, you'd be outraged!"

"Hum. Umm."

We passed a lush area of tomatoes where water sprinklers were at work.

"Just look at those tomatoes! All those sprinklers! What investment!"

I didn't answer my bewitched-by-Israeli-industry-and-achievements spouse. The Palestinians in many instances had had water diverted from their villages. A communal water tank would be made available for them from which they could draw what water they needed, but it made life intolerable for them.

Driving north as we were, I realized we must be travelling parallel with Samaria where the Samaritans, the descendants of the remnant of the lost tribes of Israel, lived.

Originally the twelve tribes of Israel had been one kingdom, united under King David and his son King Solomon. But the heavy taxation and forced labour under Solomon due to his temple-building project, caused the ten northern tribes finally to break away and appoint their rebel leader, Jeroboam, as their king.

As a separate kingdom, the people fell into idolatry. Under King Ahab and his famous wife, Jezebel, the prophet Elijah warned them of God's wrath at their falling away from worshipping God but to no avail, and Elijah had had to flee from Jezebel's fury. Ahab and Jezebel died violent deaths which, of course, was attributed to God's divine anger. The northern kingdom was finally overrun by the Assyrians in 721 B.C., the ruling classes deported, and foreigners brought in to take control. More divine retribution.

The southern kingdom of Judah, though, had also

displeased Yahweh, and they were soon clobbered in the sixth century when the Babylonians under their king, Nebuchadnezzar, invaded and took the people into exile. While grieving for the loss of their kingdom and the destruction of their holy temple, the Jews in exile began reminiscing about their historic past. They lamented their shortcomings which had so displeased Yahweh, and promised faithfully to serve him better.

To their joy, Yahweh apparently heard their prayers because in due course they were allowed to return to their land. They began to rebuild their temple, rejecting all offers of assistance in this matter from the Samaritans whom they had come to mistrust. This riled the Samaritans and, as a consequence, the latter built a temple of their own on Mount Gerizim in Samaria, a building to vie with the new one in Jerusalem. They even claimed that Abraham's son, Isaac, had been offered as a sacrifice on Mount Gerizim, not in Jerusalem, and that Adam had been created out of dust from Mount Gerizim. Today they believe themselves the only true descendents of the original twelve tribes from the Old Testament.

We passed a giant industrial plant, then palm groves and huge reservoirs. Then came a network of pylons, tall and slender industrial chimneys, oil and coal plants.

We saw the sea. Why was I surprised? Somehow I'd become so entrapped by Jerusalem and its immediate desert environs that I'd forgotten that Israel had the Mediterranean as a sea border.

We arrived at the archaeological ruins of ancient Caesarea where we were taken to the reconstructed Roman theatre. There we were given time to explore. We climbed the steps between the tiered seats, and from the top looked out to where the inky blue of the Mediterranean met the blue of the sky. A passing cruise liner looked whiter than white against the blue. The tall, slender industrial chimneys we'd passed earlier were just visible through a haze.

A few tiers from the bottom of the theatre I could see the W.I. woman and her small band of institute members. As ever she was organizing them for a photo call session. "No, can't answer that but must be Roman, I'd say. Yes, definitely Roman, you can tell by its shape. Now stop fidgeting all of you!" She retreated from them with her camera and raised it to her eye. Having taken the photo she remarked: "Just remembered Pontius Pilate was here. I read it in my guide – What? Yes, I'd love one, thanks – Somewhere around here there's a stone inscribed with his name. Don't want to miss that!"

The ancient city of Caesarea had been the brain-child of Herod the Great, built in honour of Caesar Augustus. The first century Jewish historian, Josephus, in his book, *The Jewish War*, described how, before Caesarea was built, there'd been no proper harbour in Palestine because its shoreline had no natural bays; there was no shelter from the storms which used to make the sea 'boil up'.

According to Josephus, Herod sank blocks of stone as large as fifty feet long and nine feet deep on to the sea bed, and then built a mole two hundred feet wide and a hundred feet long to break the force of the waves. Along this he erected massive towers and, at the harbour mouth, were three colossal statues. The streets of Caesarea flanked by limestone houses led to the port and, on rising ground opposite the harbour entrance, he erected a temple of Caesar Augustus. Inside was a statue of Caesar, so magnificent that it was on a par with that of the cult statue of Zeus at Olympia (one of the seven wonders of the ancient world).

To quote Josephus, Herod the Great 'by lavish expenditure and unshakable determination won the battle against nature... The site was as awkward as could be... while its (Caesarea's) beauty gave no hint of the obstacles encountered.'

Josephus, in his *The Jewish War*, mentioned practically everything regarding Jewish matters at the time, but never mentioned Jesus or the killing of the boy babies around Bethlehem. Herod wasn't so much the mad and bad king that the Christians liked to make him out to be but was Herod the Great. He'd been a prolific builder and, at one time, had been a friend of Antony and Cleopatra. In fact it had been Antony who'd recommended to Caesar that he appoint Herod king of Judaea. It was why Herod had felt a need to show his gratitude to Augustus by founding Caesarea and building a temple in his honour.

We were summoned down from the theatre to join the others. Soon the Scottish minister was reading a passage from Acts 10:24-26, about the apostle Peter coming to Caesarea where he was summoned to the house of a centurion called Cornelius. In true Scottish fashion his 'r's rang out. "'...Corrrnelius was expecting them and had called together his kinsmen and close friends. When Peter entered, Corrrnelius met him and fell down at his feet and worshiped him. But Peter lifted him up, saying, "Stand up; I too am a man."...'"

At the end of the passage he closed the Bible and repeated the words: "'I too am a man'. I want to draw your attention to these words. Because Peter performed miracles in the name of the Lord it was natural for Corrrnelius, who was a Roman, to think Peter a god. But Peter corrected him: 'I too am a man', he told him."

We stood in a circle and sang a hymn. The Scottish

minister always led the hymn-singing because he had a strong and powerful voice. He used his arm for beating a firm rhythm and bent his whole body into it. "'Brrread of heaven, Brrread of heaven...'" I noticed that the Irish girl stood with her nose up to the breeze, her eyes half closed, her lips barely moving. I didn't think she was singing.

I supposed this hymn was chosen because, on his way to Caesarea, Peter had been on the roof of a house and had fallen into a trance. He had seen something like a great sheet descend from heaven containing unclean animals. A voice had told him to eat but he had refused because it wasn't kosher, whereupon the voice had said: "'What God has cleansed, you must not call common'". In other words Peter was being told to make a break with Jewish food laws and take the Christian message to the gentiles.

Peter had only gone to Cornelius because an angel had instructed Cornelius to send for him.

"It's very odd," I said to Harry afterwards as we followed Michael who was leading the way to some other archaeological treasure, "That God never sends angels to deliver messages any more. Why do you suppose that is?"

"Don't ask me. There probably aren't any messages."

"But if there were, if somebody said 'the angel of the Lord came to me last night', wouldn't you think him rather odd? Or if he told you that he saw a sheet full of forbidden food but the Lord had told him he had cleansed it, wouldn't you raise an eyebrow?"

"People in those days weren't surprised by it so, presumably, it was admirable to have a visit from an angel, or to be spoken to by God in a dream."

"So you believe in angels?"

"Of course I do. Well, in their proper place."

"You mean in the Bible?"

"Yes."

"So if an angel came to the Canon today and he told us he'd seen one, because it wasn't in the Bible you would actually think him a bit weird?"

"Yes. No. Well. Hum."

The Irish girl caught up with us. "St. Paul came here to Caesarea," she said. "He was sent as a prisoner from Jerusalem guarded by two hundred soldiers and seventy horsemen. That's how important St. Paul was. I like St. Paul. St. Paul was never afraid. He knew he was speaking truth and wasn't afraid before the king."

"The king? Was there a king?"

"King Agrippa. He was Herod's great grandson, King Agrippa II. King Agrippa I died here because he was against God. He murdered Christians and would have murdered Peter – "

"You mean Paul?"

"No, I mean Peter. In Jerusalem. They imprisoned Peter in Jerusalem, but an angel of the Lord saved him."

"Oh, an angel – yes."

It wasn't easy to conjure up the splendour of Herod's ancient city here at Caesarea. To picture a palace once rising from today's ruins was impossible. And where was the temple of Caesar Augustus now? Unlike the evocative temples of Greece with their remaining columns and locations chosen for their sacred qualities, here everything looked a jigsaw of ruins in a flat and boring landscape enhanced only by the Mediterranean. We caught up with our group.

"Please! gather round! Here you have the stone with the name of Pontius Pilate inscribed on it."

"Oh, the stone! Gather round, girls! The stone of Pontius Pilate! Good man, Michael, I didn't want to miss that!" The W.I. woman began organizing her party, arranging them either side of the Pontius Pilate stone, before stepping back and raising her camera.

Michael told us that the stone had been discovered in the theatre where we'd just been. "It was here at Caesarea that Pontius Pilate lived," he said. "As you know, he was Roman governor of Judaea, and travelled to Jerusalem for the Jewish Passover when Jesus was condemned and crucified, a journey of sixty-four miles. Now do you have any questions?"

"Can't think of one right now, but sure to think of one later!" said the W.I. woman to her companions.

"Pontius Pilate was a murderer!" announced the Irish girl.

"Dear me, pet, he wasn't to know the consequences of his actions," murmured the eighty-seven year old.

As we walked on I said to the Canon's wife: "I've read somewhere that the Egyptian Coptic Church made Pontius Pilate a saint. Do you know anything about that? It seems very odd."

"Yes, I've heard that," she replied. As usual she was a little breathless and moved her bulk slowly and with some difficulty.

"What was that you said?" asked the Irish girl who seemed to have the radar instincts of a bat whenever some delicate religious subject was being discussed.

"We were talking about Pontius Pilate being canonized," said the Canon's wife.

"That can't be true," the Irish girl objected immediately.

"The Egyptian Church – the Coptic Church in Egypt – believes that Pontius Pilate was at heart a Christian. He never wanted our Lord to be crucified." But before she'd finished her sentence the Irish girl was gone, doing one of her circuitous walks, her shoulder-bag clutched under her arm, her nose in the air and her hair flouncing, as though the clean Mediterranean air would blow away any contamination and save her soul.

"Very unpredictable," remarked the Canon's wife.

I'd meant to ask Michael where the first early church had been, but he was now far ahead of the group leading us away from the ruins.

"Early church?" the Canon's wife looked around her when I asked her if she knew where it might be. "I know there was a Byzantine church over there near to where the temple of Augustus once stood." And she pointed to a minaret. "The Moslems replaced the early church with a mosque... And then the Crusaders replaced the mosque with a cathedral."

I remembered reading somewhere that the church in question had been built on the ruins of an ancient synagogue.

So much conflict, so much despair, so much hope. And all in the name of God.

Here we are in Tiberias. Our hotel overlooks the Sea of Galilee with the Golan Heights beyond. Magical! It's all stupifyingly peaceful in the evening light with the Golan Heights shadowed and golden. A boat with a canvas awning is chugging quietly homeward, its engine throbbing a gentle rhythm and its wake barely disturbing the calm waters.

Tiberias was founded by one of Herod the Great's sons in 18 A.D. and was named after the Emperor Tiberius. After the second Jewish revolt failed in 135 A.D. the Jews were expelled from Jerusalem and many came here where rabbis set up a centre of learning, no doubt to keep the Jewish beliefs alive for posterity.

I think I have to agree with Richard Dawkins that religion is a virus, a sickness that seems to send everyone's temperature soaring. I really don't like dogmatism – maybe I mean Godmatism (good word). Godmatism is doctrinal and demanding and impossible as it demands faith. Surely understanding and well-reasoned thinking stand head and shoulders above faith? Godmatists would disagree.

Extraordinarily, the Gnostics of the 2nd century, who were declared horrible heretics by the early Church Fathers, believed that the Jewish/Christian God was a megalomaniac and not to be worshipped. They believed that above him was the true, omnipotent, universal divine spirit, and humans had a spark within them of this divine being. Gnostics (the word means 'those who know') had an initiation ceremony to bring them to Gnosticism, to knowledge and unity with this eternal divine spirit. Trouble with all human attempts to find the truth is that they sometimes hit the nail on the head in one fleeting inspirational moment, but then elaborate, and invariably either go over the top or wide of the mark.

I'm annoyed with myself 'cos when we were in Caesarea I forgot Eusebius – Eusebius, 4th century bishop of Caesarea. And there we were in his territory – probably writing his History of the Church. It was that book which first triggered my interest in the fact that so many early saints and martyrs had names similar to the old Olympian gods – it seemed to me that over the centuries pagans had gradually been subtly persuaded that their gods had become Christian! Dionysos became St. Dionysios, Demeter, St. Demetrios – there'd even been a Zeus who'd died a Christian martyr. Fascinating!

And I also forgot about Origen who in the 3rd century lived at Caesarea for twenty years or so, having founded a Christian academy there. He it was who wrote Contra Celsus *when Celsus (whom Godmatists must have positively loathed) wrote his satirical attacks on the Christians which have always left me feeling slightly guilty because they've made me laugh. Celsus wanted to know why it was that in every other religion anyone wanting to be initiated into it was expected to have lived exemplary lives, but for Christians they welcomed sinners, the unwise and wretches. Origen, of course, being a Godmatist had to have the last word and said that the Church encouraged sinners, children and wretches because those were the people who most needed guidance in order to be brought to God. You could never win with Origen!*

Anyway, here we are in Tiberias now.

On the way here we must have passed within a few miles of Kibbutz Deganiah where the young Moshe Dayan (of later eye-patch fame) was born and spent most of his childhood. Amazing man with his black eye-patch – he lost his eye when a bullet shattered the field glasses he was using. For a lesser person it would have been the end of everything, but not him! He had enormous dash and daring, and was a super-humanly energetic and decisive charismatic leader who led the Israelis to victory when all seemed almost certain defeat. Apparently, when he was a boy growing up in the kibbutz the Jews of Deganiah got on well with their neighbouring Arab farmers and attended each others festivals. It wasn't until Jewish immigration escalated, when the Jews positively flooded in after World War II that the troubles began. When he was fourteen Moshe D enrolled in the Jewish secret underground resistance, the Haganah. It was the time of the British Mandate when it was illegal for anyone to possess an unlicensed weapon, or for Jews to have military training in order to defend themselves. For Moshe Dayan such British dictates were simply things to be ignored if the Zionist dream was to be achieved. Just like Alexander the Great, he never gave in to obstacles but found a way to overcome them.

He positively relished a challenge!

Harry's telling me it's seven o'clock – supper time. Have to stop and tidy up, I suppose –

Two hours later. The dining-room was full of pilgrim groups, seated at separate tables. Each table had on it the flag of the country from which the group had come. Some stood and sang a short hymn, or said a prayer before helping themselves from the service table and sitting down to eat.

I found myself sitting beside the Irish girl. I'm amused by her because she is so unusual. Tonight she was totally bonkers. She suddenly whispered and nodded her head indicating one of the waiters behind the serving table, and asked if I didn't think him 'gorgeous'? The waiter in question was quite a nice looking fellow who looked more Arab than Jewish – Egyptian, perhaps? She was in confidential mood and her eyes positively sparkled. She wanted me to suggest a way for her to meet him. I told her that in the old days when a girl fancied a young man she'd drop her lace handkerchief at his feet, and if he was chivalrous he'd pick it up. She didn't have one, she said, only a tissue. Well – how about dropping her table napkin instead, I suggested? Eyes still sparkling, she said she didn't want him to think her 'daft'. So I then suggested (must have been the wine) that she drop her plate of food at his feet. That way he'd have to do something.She got very excited at this, and unfortunately the eighty-seven year old overheard and gave me one of her 'Ooooh, pet!' gentle admonishments. She then told the Canon's wife who threw me a strongly disapproving look of rebuke, so I'm in the doghouse. The Irish girl must have done something, though I don't know what, because on our way back to my room I saw her talking to the 'gorgeous' one in a very animated way. 'Would she, wouldn't she' was written all over her face. Did she or didn't she is something I probably will never know.

Tomorrow we're destined for Nazareth. That'll be interesting! Why will it be interesting? Because the Gospels say that Jesus grew up there. But, as I don't really believe in God, how can I believe in the Son? So why, then, am I looking forward to going to Nazareth? I suppose it has to be because I was, as Richard Dawkins would say, innoculated (or do I mean indoctrinated) with Christian stories as a child. That's what's interesting!

CHAPTER

8

NAZARETH

The principal of the school we were visiting in Nazareth looked harassed as he spoke to us about the problems faced by Arab Palestinian Christian Israelis. Yes, you can have all four identities at once, he said. His father had grown up with all four labels at the time of the British Mandate. When the State of Israel had finally been proclaimed in 1948, the family had fled to Lebanon. At that time Ben Gurion had been Prime Minister and had little time or sympathy for the Palestinian Arabs, asserting that they'd shown no interest in their land before, and would be perfectly 'at home' in any Arab country. In other words, let them flee what was now Israel and make their homes elsewhere.

"In the West," went on the principal of the school, "they think that if someone is an Arab then he lives in the desert. When I was in the U.S. in 1989 they thought that because I was Arab I must be uneducated and live in a tent."

The poor man seemed highly agitated, a coiled spring of energy ready to leap off in one direction or another. He hadn't been expecting us and chairs had been hastily set around a small area in an open hallway through which staff and pupils passed continually; some sat at tables along one wall. Someone had an urgent word in his ear, and he gave instructions before picking up the thread of his thoughts and continuing with what seemed to be a know-it-all-by-heart exposition.

"We have been here in Nazareth since the very first Arab Christians of the first century," he declared. "This is a Christian school but most of the students in the school are Moslem. We have two teachers who are Jewish. Each day we begin with Christian prayers but we do not impose our Christianity on the children. They come to us because they know they will receive a good education. If we can live together peacefully as a community in this school, then it is difficult to understand how it is that we cannot live equally peacefully outside the school.

"But we cannot. Here in Nazareth we have many, many problems. There are very many different Christian denominations in the town. As Christians we were once in the majority but now it is the Moslems who are in the majority. This poses many problems among Palestinian Arabs which is to the benefit of the Israelis." He sprang up to give a member of staff who was passing some instructions, then returned to his seat and continued.

"We have here the Christian sites and what you will see will look good, but under the surface it is bad. Nazareth is a dead city. After six in the evening everything is closed and there is nothing for our young people. To have nothing for them makes life impossible and frustrating for them. Many families here do not have water or heating. But for the Jews, they have Illit Nazareth, a settlement on the east of Nazareth where they have everything – water, heating, swimming-pools, cinemas and evening entertainment. It is very hard being here and knowing that the Jews want us to leave. But this is our home and has been for generations before the time of the birth of Jesus. Why should we leave?

"There is much unemployment…" His mobile rang and he excused himself as he got up. He paced around in circles for a while as he listened briefly and replied curtly before switching off and returning to his seat.

"Excuse me. As you see we are very busy." He passed a harassed hand over his face, then gathered his thoughts. "Yes, life here in Nazareth is full of difficulties. I can tell you the story of a Moslem who hanged himself because the competitiveness of life here was too much for him. He had been unable to earn a living to keep his family. His son found him. Can you imagine that?

"I tell you now about my grandfather who returned to Nazareth from the Lebanon in 1958. My family had just enough money to buy a car for him so he could work as a taxi driver. The Israelis said he must take a driving test, and this he did and he passed the test. But to license the car as a taxi was too costly so he had to drive illegally to make a little money.

"One of my relatives had her property bulldozed to make a road for the Jews up to their new settlement called Illit Nazareth. One day my relative was brave and snatched the watch of a Jew and she was at once called a thief. But she replied that why should he make a fuss when she had only stolen a watch but his people had stolen her home?

"This is the unfairness that we have to endure. The Jews say they themselves have the right to return, the Arabs have no right to return and, if they do, they find their property razed to the ground or else occupied.

"But as Christians we are ambassadors for peace. The

Israelis should be building bridges, not ugly walls. We can only pray that we, as living Christians, can put right what is wrong here in the Holy Land where freedom fighters are called terrorists. We have to try by peaceful means to put right all the injustices that we are made to suffer. We have to work towards a peaceful solution by prayer and faith until the Israelis recognize that, unless there is equality as they promised us in their Declaration of Independence in 1948, there will never be peace for them here in Israel. There can only be peace when there is justice."

He was told by a secretary that somebody was waiting to see him. He glanced at his watch and apologized for having to leave immediately. There was no opportunity to ask questions and the Canon quickly thanked him for finding time to speak to us.

His words had put us in the picture about Nazareth. Before walking down the hill from the school, we paused on the school terrace to look out over the city. Nazareth was a conglomeration of flat-roofed houses and straggling high-rise apartment blocks which fanned outwards from the central imposing cream coloured Basilica of the Annunciation with its gigantic grey cupola. The basilica marked the site said to have been the home of Mary and Joseph.

"You know," I said to Harry as we walked down from the school into Nazareth, "that it's been suggested by those who've made a study of the matter that Nazareth actually never existed at the time of Joseph and Mary. It was never mentioned in the Old Testament, or the Talmud, or early rabbinical literature. It sort of grew magically from – well, from the Gospels."

"Well, I don't believe that somehow."

"According to one source, excavations have revealed

that there were many tombs here and it was probably a burial ground which, of course, always had to be outside inhabited areas. One theory is that the word 'Nazareth' or 'Jesus the Nazarene' – might have come from the Hebrew root letters NZR which could have been mis-translated from 'Nazara' meaning 'Truth'. So the 'Annunciation' which Christians claim happened here, happened somewhere in 'Truth' – got it?"

"Hum."

We were by now being rushed through the bazaar which seemed a real shame, but I supposed Michael knew it was best to hurry past the Moslem vendors. We emerged from the covered souq, and passed Turkish houses in urgent need of restoration. A little further and we were in the centre of Nazareth where Christian sites were preserved for pilgrims to feast their religious imaginations on.

"I have another theory, of course," I told Harry as we hurried along with the others. "The Arabic for carpenter is *'najjār'*. Well, in Greek there's no such letter as 'J' but 'tz' would be the equivalent. Therefore, *natzār* would be the Greek way of writing the Arabic word *'najjār'* – and the Gospels were written in Greek, don't forget – which explains why Joseph of Nazareth was said to be a carpenter – *natzār*. Do you understand what I mean?" But I doubted if my attempt at a theory would stand up to academic scrutiny. I just found the thought interesting that Joseph had been given the role of a carpenter because he came from Nazareth, or else Nazareth (which apparently hardly existed at the time) had been given the name because Joseph, a carpenter, had come there.

We were led into the Greek Orthodox Church of St. Gabriel built beside a well, known as Mary's Well. The interior of the church was mystical with its muted lighting and its frescoed walls and columns supporting a barrel-roof from which hung numerous icon lamps and chandeliers. It had magnificent carved and gilded central doors to its sanctuary screen. I would have liked to have spent time in the church ruminating. Instead, we were led on to an ancient building built by the Crusaders but whose walls had on them ceramic plaques of Islamic geometric design, suggesting a Moslem occupation at some stage. At its far end were narrow stone steps going down to Mary's Well.

The well was where it was said the angel Gabriel had come to Mary and told her she'd found favour with God and was to immaculately conceive – a highly worrying thing for a young unmarried girl. But Mary accepted it quietly and managed to explain away her predicament to Joseph to whom she was betrothed. Joseph, fortunately, was also helped by God who sent Gabriel to tell him not to be dismayed by Mary's condition because she'd conceived by the Holy Spirit. I could imagine the reaction of a man in this day and age if his fiancée came up with this piece of news proclaimed by an angel. Joseph must have been a saint with no doubts as to his betrothed's innocence. The Gospel writers said it fulfilled somewhat curious Old Testament prophecy.

The Jews, whose prophecies Christians declared had been fulfilled with the coming of Christ, didn't go along with the Christian nativity story. There'd been no angel Gabriel announcing that she'd conceived by the Holy Spirit. Instead, the Jewish story was that she had been seduced by a Roman soldier.

The Moslems, however, were much more sensitive towards the Christian version. Muhammad had met both Jews and Christians while living in Mecca and then Medina, and had himself been enlightened by God regarding the birth of Jesus. In the Koran it says: '...she (Mary) left her people and betook herself to a solitary place to the east. We (God) sent to her Our spirit in the semblance of a full-grown man. And when she saw him she said: "May the Merciful defend me from you!..."' (Sura 19). The man had then informed her that she was to bear a child by immaculate conception.

To continue with the Sura in the Koran. Having given birth Mary came back to her people and they were dismayed and shocked by the sight of her with a baby. But Jesus (as a baby) spoke from his cradle, describing himself as 'the servant of God' and a prophet. I wondered whether that wasn't an echo from the birth of Apollo (conceived by Zeus) who as a baby was reported to have said: '"...I will utter to men the unerring counsel of Zeus"'. (Homer's *Hymn to Apollo*).

Sura 19 goes on to explain that Jesus is not the son of God but the son of Mary. To quote: 'That is the whole truth, which they (Christians) still doubt. God forbid that He Himself should beget a son! When He decrees a thing He need only say: "Be," and it is.'

I couldn't resist the remark: "Be and it is!"

"Be what?" Harry enquired.

"That's what the Koran says God can do – i.e. getting Mary pregnant. I wonder why he doesn't say 'Be!' to everything that displeases him so that it becomes good."

"It's because he wants to see you BEing and working towards what HE wants, I imagine."

"Why?"

But I got no response, so went on: "You know, of course, that they say Plato was the result of a virgin birth with Apollo supposedly his father? Great people are sometimes given these strange birth stories. Alexander the Great was another. According to Origen in his *Contra Celsus* God tried this virgin birth magic with certain animals before trying it on humans. Vultures, for example. Female vultures just produce. When God says 'Be' so they be. Amazing!"

"What you have to realize is that what you see is just a fraction of the whole picture," Harry remarked stolidly.

That was an astonishing thought! That every individual could only see what was within his or her own narrow intellectual purview. It was astonishing also to realize that no human in the whole world could ever see the complete world picture at any one moment, only glimpses at a time. The cleverest of men and the most powerful could only read a book line by line or page by page, he could never read the whole at a glance. The human mind was really quite limited in its capacity. The brain could absorb a great deal but a person could only speak one thought at a time; humans could only think in slither-like portions of their entire knowledge at any one moment.

"Such a pity that the city of Nazareth was destroyed by the Romans during the first Jewish revolt," the Canon's wife remarked as we walked along together to the Synagogue Church.

I wasn't going to blab my latest discoveries that far from being a city at the time of Jesus (as reported in Matthew and Luke) it had been of so little significance that no other writers had mentioned it until the fourth century (except in the Gospels) – and this was despite the listing of sixty-three towns in Galilee mentioned in the Talmud and forty-five cities in Galilee mentioned by Josephus.

"To be walking on the ground that our Lord walked is humbling. I feel so privileged, so fortunate."

As we approached the towering mass of the Basilica of the Annunciation, she told me how Saladin had conquered

Nazareth in the twelfth century which was then recaptured by the Crusaders in the thirteenth.

We were joined by the Scottish minister whose energy and exuberance seemed to spur the Canon's wife to a slightly faster pace.

"Did you get some water from Mary's Well?" she asked him. He slipped her a bottle which she put into her handbag. "Good man! When you're in my condition you'll try anything."

"We all believe in miracles," declared the minister cheerfully. "I've my own wee bottle in case of need. It was a shame the Moslems scuttled the Christian millennium plans for this city," he remarked.

"I suppose it was to be expected," said the Canon's wife.

"Och aye. It was predictable."

"Why, what happened?" I asked.

"Did you not read about it? Plans were drawn up in the early nineteen nineties to transform Nazareth and put in place facilities for the millennium for the thousands of pilgrims expected to come to celebrate the birth of our Lord here. It was to have been good for Nazareth and good for the Israeli economy. But the Islamic extremists became jealous and declared the square in front of the Basilica 'waqf', meaning the land was Moslem endowment property. They put up a dirty great tent in front of the entrance to the Basilica as a provisional mosque, and said they wanted to build a minaret and mosque a hundred metres high. The intention was to dwarf the Basilica church."

"It was all very unfortunate," the Canon's wife remarked.

"It was more than unfortunate," exclaimed the Scottish minister. "The Moslems put up their tent three days before Christmas."

"What was upsetting was having the Moslems praying

five times a day right there at the entrance to the Basilica."

"Too right!"

"Especially when they celebrated their festivals," put in the Canon's wife.

"Och aye, they did that with a vengeance too. A few weeks after putting up their tent in time for Christmas they were celebrating their *Eid al-Fitr* festival on the disputed ground. That was a three-day affair marking the end of Ramadan."

I could imagine the scene and the jollifications as the Moslems celebrated the festival with the first sighting of the new moon marking the end of their one month of fasting.

Ramadan was the month in which Muhammad was first enlightened with the words of the Koran. Towards the end of Ramadan *Laylat al-Qadr* (Night of Power) is of particular significance as it commemorates the day on which the angel Gabriel first came to Muhammad and ordered him to recite the words of the Koran which then became engraved on his heart.

"But surely the Israeli authorities could have stopped the Moslems wrecking the Christian plans for the millennium?" I asked.

"The Israelis! They work on a 'divide and rule' policy! It suited them just fine to have the Moslem and Christian Palestinians at each other's throats!"

"You'd have thought they'd want the best for Nazareth to bring in revenue from the pilgrims," I put in.

"They want that, right enough, but they – the Israelis – want the whole lot out, that's what the Israelis want."

"They have Illit Nazareth," added the Canon's wife. "They're all right up there with their government buildings and their comfortable life styles."

I was becoming more and more bemused by these wheels within wheels of political and religious intrigue. It wasn't enough for the Palestinians to unite because of their race. Their religion (either Moslem or Christian) took priority over everything else, just as Jewishness, according to Jews, qualified them to claim Palestinian territory.

We arrived before the Basilica of the Annunciation. It was a grandiose building built on a grandiose scale in a grandiose plaza. Its cupola rose from its centre like a gigantic grey stub of a pencil with a cream-coloured adornment around its base and another around its point on which stood a huge lantern, Light of the World symbol.

This majestic basilica was consecrated in 1969 and is said to have been the fifth church built over the grotto, the site of the small house where tradition has it the Holy Family lived. It was yet again Constantine's aged mother doing her tour of the Holy Land who'd identified the site. Her diligence and stamina were spectacular. I supposed both she and her son knew that pilgrims would come flocking from all corners of the world because Christianity was in 'tongues' and, therefore, worldwide. Besides, Helena was possibly keen on seeking forgiveness of her own sins. Rumour has it she was the daughter of an inn keeper and had been a prostitue before rising to the dizzy heights of becoming the mother of the Emperor Constantine, whose father might or might not have been married to her. She probably identified herself with the woman who was a sinner and who wept and annointed Jesus' feet with ointment (Luke 7:37) and whom Jesus forgave (Luke 7:48).

Michael drew our attention to the massive bronze entrance doors depicting the important points of Christian belief: the fall of Adam, the fulfilment of prophecy and the main events of the life of Jesus.

Christians and Jews blamed Adam for the Fall with all its gloomy consequences. The Moslems, on the other hand, regard Adam's disobedience as having been forgiven by God because Adam repented. It was Satan alone who was responsible for the evils of the world. It all came about when Satan (he'd been one of God's angels) had refused to bow down to God's new creation (Adam) the first man made from clay, of whom God was very proud.

I pointed out Adam on the bronze door and told Harry the Moslem story.

"If God hadn't demanded that all his angels bow down to him there wouldn't have been any trouble in the world," I said.

"Is that what he wanted Satan to do?"

"Yes, according to the Moslems. But Satan refused, declaring himself superior to Adam because he, Satan, had been created out of fire and Adam only of clay."

"Did the other angels bow down to Adam?"

"Yes. They were obedient. But God was so annoyed with Satan that he cast him out of heaven, whereupon Satan was furious and said that because of it he would for ever lie in ambush and lead men astray. That's why he tempted Adam to eat the fruit of the tree of knowledge when God had expressly forbidden it. Can you imagine life without knowledge and a bit of sin thrown in? It'd be very dull."

We were led into the interior of the Basilica. It was unlike any church I'd ever seen, with massive girder-like supports as though carrying a massive flyover into a city. The altar and sanctuary were on a lower level, centrally placed and surrounded by seats. The whole area containing the table-like stone altar was cordoned off from the main body of the church by a decorative metal railing.

Looking up to the towering cupola from inside was like looking up into a giant gathering together of cream coloured paper darts extending upwards to the lantern. It was supposed to represent a Madonna lily and was fifty-five metres high. No wonder the Christians were upset on learning that their grandiose Basilica church was to be dwarfed by a Moslem mosque whose minaret would be nearly twice the height. The final plans for building the mosque, in fact, were never implemented.

We were given time to wander around, and Harry and I sat and watched a Mass being celebrated. With time and solitude and silence the immensity of the place grew on me and I found that, instead of rather disliking it, there was, in fact, something extraordinarily powerful and majestic about it. It had a ponderous sort of dignity with its grey concrete pylons. The whole structure demanded admiration.

We were summoned to go down to the Grotto where tradition has it Mary and Joseph lived with the child Jesus. This was also claimed to have been where the angel Gabriel had come and told Mary she would immaculately conceive – the other location being Mary's Well.

Whatever its past history, I got no sense of anything having happened there. I had been able to visualize an angel at Mary's Well, but not here. Here they were trying to make a claim to something which, by its sheer magnitude of stone and concrete stifled the mind so the spirit couldn't get lift-off.

I wondered why, if other great figures had been given virgin births, Muhammad hadn't been. His father had died soon after his marriage to his mother who was already pregnant with him. One day she heard a voice telling her that the son she would have would be the ruler and prophet of his people. Apparently, when Muhammad was born, a brilliant light shone over the whole world from east to west. Legend has it he was born circumcized, and with the navel cord already cut. At his birth he fell from his mother to the ground where he took a handful of sand and gazed heavenwards.

The strange thing about Muhammad was that he was never said to be divine like Jesus but was wholly human. He married, had eleven wives and two concubines, had two (maybe three) sons who all died in infancy, and four daughters, two of whom died before he did. On his death he was buried and that was that. There were no sightings of him afterwards, no resurrection. His life and death were the same as any normal man.

When we left the Basilica of the Annunciation I found myself walking alongside the Canon's wife yet again, but this time the Canon too stalked along beside us, a tall, thin, slightly bent figure. Rightly or wrongly I found myself saying: "It's odd that no one today claims descent from Jesus. Yet Muhammad had descendants through his daughters."

"Had he? I've no idea," said the Canon's wife.

"There was James, the brother of Our Lord, but he died a martyr," the Canon remarked.

He walked along, bending his head to hear what we were saying. His lean face and sad eyes were gentle and I felt he was approachable. I said: "Jesus didn't start his teaching until he was thirty. That was really very odd, wasn't it?" There was a polite cough as the Canon considered a reply but, in fact, found nothing sensible to say so remained silent. I went on: "At the time of Jesus, or so I understand, most Jewish men were expected to marry at eighteen. So maybe Jesus married?" There was another polite cough. "In comparison there was no mystery around Muhammad. All his life is accounted for – infancy, childhood, marriage to the widow Khadija, her death and then his other wives."

The Canon's wife said: "I'm afraid we know little about Islam."

The Canon said: "What was that?"

His wife shouted: "She was asking about Our Lord's family. There is little about it in the Gospels, dear."

"They trace his lineage from King David," remarked the Canon somewhat unhelpfully.

"She means from Jesus onwards, dear. Like Muhammad, she's comparing the life of Our Lord with the life of Muhammad."

The Canon shook his head sadly and remarked: "I know very little about Muhammad."

I didn't persevere and a veil of silence fell over us.

Soon we were on the coach and on our way back to Tiberias.

★

I am sitting – maybe lounging is a better word – on the hotel terrace beside the Sea of Galilee. There is a very tranquil evening light. I've just seen a black sea bird skimming the surface of the water. The Golan Heights are gold and shadowed in the far distance.

Nazareth? Well!!!!! Seething with frustrated Christian/ Moslem citizens, with the Jews cheering from the sidelines or, rather, from the top of their hill settlement. Can't think why these God-religions don't enjoy each others festivals and take part in them instead of trying to wreck them. Most peculiar. If they play football, or play in an orchestra, they don't think about each others religions.

Quite surprised that the Canon and his wife knew nothing about Islam. Suppose it's not important to them. Glad I didn't point out that God was odd to enlighten Christians with the Trinity idea and crucifixion and Resurrection etc., and then enlightened Muhammad with different facts. Wonder what they'd have said to that if I'd mentioned it?

Passed a man with two women sitting out by the swimming-pool here earlier – the man was stocky, middle-aged with receding grey hair drawn back in a pony tail. One of the women was enveloped in black and might have been a novice nun. I'd noticed them singing some sort of chant before supper yesterday and found them fascinating. I've discovered they're from America and are Russian Orthodox.

As an atheist and evolutionist how does Richard Dawkins explain consciousness – the human ability to remember the past, to plan for the future, to think of things that cannot be seen or touched, the spiritual, mystical, ethereal and all that? He needs to write another book to explain it! But perhaps he has and I've missed it.

Time for bed. All sorts of exciting things tomorrow – Mt. Tabor where the Transfiguration took place, and then the Golan Heights. Looking forward to that.

THE TRANSFIGURATION - ARMAGEDDON

CHAPTER

9

MT. TABOR, MEGIDDO AND THE GOLAN HEIGHTS

I sat beside the taxi driver who was taking us up Mount Tabor. He was a Bedouin and I wanted to ask him what his experiences of living in Israel were. Instead, I quizzed him on the safer subject of family. With pride he said he had ten children who were now all grown up and were doctors, bankers and teachers. I couldn't believe (and didn't believe) that such a grizzled looking Bedouin could have spawned such a tribe of professionals.

"And I have twenty-seven grandchildren," said the old rogue. That I could believe.

As we neared the summit he waved a hand towards the plain below and said: "Megiddo."

"Megiddo? Armageddon?"

"Armageddon," he rasped.

Armageddon! So that was where it was said the final battle would be fought!

Michael led us to the Church of the Transfiguration. The first church on Mount Tabor had been built by St. Cyril of Jerusalem in 348 A.D. at which time, no doubt, the Christian message of love, forgiveness and peace was getting around. But then had come the Moslems (who also believed in submission and peace) followed by the Crusaders, then the Moslems again under Saladin. So fanatical had the Crusaders become that, like the Moslem suicide-bombers of today, they also believed that by giving their lives to recapture Jerusalem and the Holy Land, they would become martyrs and go straight to heaven.

The present Church of the Transfiguration was built by the Franciscans in 1924. It was of marble with twin towers flanking an impressive entrance way. There was a mystical airiness to its interior. The altar was down several steps and above it was a glorious, glistening gold and white mosaic of the transfiguration of Christ. Beyond it was a recessed arch with a stained-glass window in rich hues of red, blue, gold and white, depicting two peacocks on either side of a chalice.

We were led down a stairway to the crypt. Under glass was displayed a portion of the honey-coloured natural rock of Mount Tabor on which the church was built. This was said to be the actual location of the transfiguration itself. The rock under the glass was strewn with scraps of paper scrawled with intercessionary prayers. Among them was a photo of a young boy. I wondered who he was. Was his family praying for some miraculous cure? Had he died? Was he some Christian Palestinian's lost child? If enough people prayed, did political situations and personal calamities change? Or did this merely ease the tormented minds of sufferers when disasters had to be endured?

I had recently read an autobiography, *Blood Brothers,* by Elias Chacour, a Palestinian Christian. He was a very remarkable man, the youngest son of a deeply devout family. They lived in a village called Biram, not far north from where we were. His father believed in forgiveness and non-violence.

In 1948, when the British relinquished the Mandate of Palestine and the new State of Israel was proclaimed, life for the Chacours had gone on much as usual. They had continued tending their orchards and harvesting their figs as they had always done. They hadn't expected trouble as they'd always lived alongside Jews and could see no reason to make enemies of them in the future. One day, however, Israeli soldiers had come to their village and several had been billeted in the Chacour house.

With traditional Arab courtesy and hospitality, Elias Chacour's father had welcomed the soldiers to his home. Though the soldiers had held themselves aloof they had behaved politely, and life had continued much as ever for the family.

All went well until one day a bullish Israeli military commander had arrived and announced that the villagers were in grave danger and they were all to leave the village for a few days. A few days only, he'd assured them, and he would personally see to it that the Israeli soldiers took good care of their homes in their absence. Trusting the word of the officer, they had departed to the hills where they had slept under the stars. But the few days had stretched to considerably longer, and eventually the elders of the village had returned to enquire when they could come back. To their dismay, when they came to the village, they found the doors to their homes smashed and their possessions vandalized.

The realization that they had been duped had been a devastating blow, and they'd had no alternative but to find shelter in another abandoned village. There they'd led a hand to mouth existence until (again without warning) the Israeli army had arrived and had ordered all the men to assemble in the village square. Elias Chacour's father and three older brothers had been taken away in lorries with no explanation given. It had left a profound impression on the young Elias whose mother and the rest of his family had now to scavenge for food in order to survive.

Nine or ten months later Elias Chacour's father and brothers had reappeared in the night, haggard and emaciated from living rough. They had been dumped by the Israelis on the Lebanese borders. Having always extended hospitality to strangers, they had soon learned that others were not of the same disposition. During their months of wanderings they had been repeatedly turned away by people and had been forced to live a vagabond existence.

In time Elias' father learned that his orchards had been commandeered by the Israelis and an Israeli kibbutz was being planned. In other words he was dispossessed. In order to earn a living at all he found his best option was to work as a labourer for the Israelis in his own beloved orchards. To remain dignified in the face of these adversities he turned to prayer; remarkably, he asked God to forgive and bless the Israelis. As a Christian, I supposed he would have known that in the Old Testament God had given his Jews this 'promised land'. His deliberate policy of acquiescence was his way of ensuring that his violent feelings of resentment were kept under control; they didn't erupt and overwhelm him. He disciplined himself to regard the whole tragedy as God's will and, in time, he believed God would hear his prayers and put right the undoubted wrongs that had been inflicted on him.

I had been outraged by the story. How could such an appalling political situation have been allowed to arise in the first place? And in the pious belief that God's will was being fulfilled? I was enraged by such belief.

We left the crypt and followed Michael out to the south side of the church where we stood beside the ruins of the original fourth century church.

From there we looked down to the panoramic view of the plain of Jezreel. Megiddo was pointed out, though it was barely visible through a haze. Clearly seen, though, was the nearer sweep of cultivated land and two huge circles divided into segments of different colours, a quite unnecessary agricultural design but, nevertheless, an artistic feat.

We stood around the Canon who read from Matthew 17 about the transfiguration: 'Jesus took with him Peter and James and John his brother, and led them up a high mountain apart. And he was transfigured before them, and his face shone like the sun, and his garments became white as light. And behold, there appeared to them Moses and Elijah, talking with him... a bright cloud overshadowed them, and a voice from the cloud said, "This is my beloved Son, with whom I am well pleased; listen to him..."' The passage continued with Jesus asking his disciples to tell no man about what they had witnessed until '"the Son of man is raised from the dead."'

The W.I. woman was standing a little way from us with her camera held against her stomach. Her white hair frothed around her cheerful face like the crest of waves. She smiled at me.

"Couldn't resist taking photographs of you all listening to the reading," she remarked. "Very moving."

"It's not the only high mountain claimed for the transfiguration," I remarked. "I think Mt. Hebron was another."

"Oh, very likely. Wouldn't really matter where it took place. S'long as we have it in the Gospels," she replied. "I grant you it's nice to think it all happened here. Rather!"

She turned and waved an arm at the Jezreel plain. "Trying to identify what crops those are. By golly, they must have taken trouble to get that design!"

The Irish girl came up and pointed towards the plain. "That's where it will all happen. Armageddon," she said.

"I jolly well hope not!"

"The final battle between good and evil. I expect it will be a nuclear bomb," she said.

"Ha, ha, ha, we certainly don't want that!"

"Well, it looks very peaceful at the moment," I remarked.

"They've had a lot of wars down there," went on the Irish girl. "Megiddo is at the cross roads of trading routes. There have always been battles down there. The Last Days won't be long now. Then the return of Our Lord..."

I meant to stay uncontroversial but the words popped out: "Jesus said that before a generation had passed he would return again, but he didn't."

"He meant his Church would come. Our Lord returned but not in the way that was expected."

"Then why do they keep expecting the Second Coming now?" I asked.

"Yes, why, indeed!" joked the W.I. woman, her eyes flitting from me to the Irish girl and back, relishing the possibility of sparks flying.

"Because Jesus will come again."

"But you've just said he has come again," I said.

"That was his Church that came. You have to believe God's word," she said. "You have to believe Scripture!" And, before anything more could be said, she'd marched away on one of her circuits.

"Golly, that was sudden!" the W.I. woman exclaimed.

She caught sight of her friends. "I've been trying out my new camera on this vista," she called out as she approached them. "Interesting to see what comes out – if anything!"

I wondered if the Irish girl was a Christian Zionist. I'd read something about them and knew they were fanatical supporters of the new State of Israel. Christian Zionists said it was the duty of all who believed in the word of God to help fulfil the prophecies, and bring about God's divine plan. They had charismatic leaders who used the media and talked of God's love for 'you – YOU!' pointing a finger towards the millions of viewers throughout the world.

One of these charismatic Bible thumpers announced that the time would be very soon when all would see the Mount of Olives on television where 'my Saviour is going to put His foot down when He comes back to earth... every eye is going to behold Him...' He was saying this at a time when the Mount of Olives was being televized. 'We will see prophecy being fulfilled right in front of our eyes!'

One of them had written a succession of books on the End of Days as prophesied in Scripture. St. John in Revelation, he wrote, had been a visionary witnessing our times, but he'd been unable to use the language of today, hence his 'locusts' were clearly today's helicopters, and the 'bow' wielded by the Antichrist referred to today's long-range missiles.

Through their media appeals these Christian Zionists raised considerable sums of money to support the new State of Israel. There was money set aside to finance the rebuilding of the temple. The blowing up of the Dome of the Rock was permissible if, in consequence, the third temple could be built. War with the Moslem countries was to be encouraged in order to bring about the Last Days.

I saw the Canon approaching. "Wonderful view," he

said pleasantly, extending an arm in order to move us all on. "It's not easy to imagine Armageddon and the final clashing of cultures, or the end of the world looking down there now," he went on.

"I wish I could understand the idea of Armageddon," I said. I thought that if anyone could explain it in a calm and reasoned manner he could.

The Canon gave a gentle cough which I was learning was a sign of ecclesiastical uncertainty, a playing-for-time way of gathering thoughts for a suitable answer.

"I always think that the idea of Armageddon serves as a useful warning to mankind of what might happen if diplomacy is allowed to fail," he remarked.

We walked back to the coach together, but I could think of nothing sensible to say in response to his uncontroversial words of wisdom.

In the book about Christian Zionism it had a passage which I'd thought alarming: 'Peace talks are... not only a waste of time, they demonstrate at best a lack of faith and at worst a rebellious defiance towards God's plans...'

On the coach I thought again about Elias Chacour's book *Blood Brothers*. He himself had always had a religious side to his nature and his father, seeing that his son was prone to going off on his own to speak to what he called his 'Champion' (Jesus), had gone to his bishop to see if he could advise him regarding Elias' education. The bishop took the matter up, and at the age of twelve Elias had been sent to an orphanage in Haifa where he'd received the education his father had wanted for him. This had prepared him for his chosen career in the Church.

One day while still at the orphanage, one of his brothers had come to see him to tell him the latest news from home. The Biram villagers had learned to their joy that the Supreme Court of Israel, had granted them permission to return to their village, and they were to be allowed back on Christmas day. This had seemed to them the most wonderful of Christmas presents, and the miracle Elias Chacour's father had been praying for daily – at last God had heard his prayers.

On Christmas morning they set off for their village singing a Christmas hymn but, when they reached the crest of the hill and looked down, to their horror they saw their village surrounded by tanks, army trucks and bulldozers. As soon as they were spotted on the hill by the soldiers, the order was given for the destruction to begin. The villagers could only watch in disbelief as their homes and their church were systematically demolished. Wooden structures were ignited, fires raged and walls and buildings collapsed. Their prayers had not been answered at all. It was a calamity.

Another book I'd read, this one on Jewish fundamentalism, had claimed that what might appear to be confiscated land once owned by Arabs was not theft but Jewish sanctification of it.

The only comment I received from Harry when I exploded these Jewish and Christian fundamentalist beliefs, and the reality of what was happening to the Palestinian Arabs was that, as I couldn't do anything about it, to stop meddling in fundamental issues.

Everyone wanted a photo of the Syrian tank on the Golan Heights. In fact it was only the upper half of a tank, the gun-turret or something, but it still looked menacing – well, exciting really, as it was more of a toy for us to examine at close quarters than a weapon. On it was scrawled messages in Arabic, *'Allahu akbar'* being the only two words I could read and understand ('God is great'). Presumably, before its capture, it had been out to kill Israelis and destroy Israel. All we'd seen on the road along the ridge of the Golan Heights had been squashed hedgehogs and the occasional dead rabbit. We really couldn't make the connection with the fact that not so long ago there'd been mutilated bodies of dead or wounded Syrian and Israeli soldiers lying along this ridge.

Michael pointed towards the east, to the sweeping vista which faded into haze, and told us we were looking into Syria. Israel's victory over this newly acquired territory was an extraordinary Israeli feat of dash and daring and, in the 1967 Six Day War, they'd even extended their country's boundaries. Their triumphs had been so miraculous that it had been compared to the Exodus and the parting of the Red Sea.

So many imaginative legends have seeped from the distant past into the human psyche to fasten like barnacles to it, that they've become part of Israeli existence itself. It is why, when an army fights and wins battles, it is imagined that God has favoured the victors and has assisted.

Yet one side's victory is another side's defeat. As I'd once said to Harry, it was odd that people continued to put their faith in God who might or might not help them to victory. It was like persisting with an erratic electrical gadget which sometimes works for you but as often doesn't.

The Yom Kippur War of October 1973, for example, had been one of the greatest triumphs in modern Israeli history – the electrical gadget had worked well for the Jews on that occasion, but had, despite the equal belief and faith of the Moslem Syrians and Egyptians, failed to function for them. The Syrians in the north where we now were, together with the Egyptians in the south, had been intent on wiping the State of Israel (the land given to God's 'chosen people') off the map of Palestine.

The 1973 war had been launched by the Syrians and Egyptians on Israel's most sacred day of the Jewish year, Yom Kippur. Yom Kippur is Hebrew for 'Day of Atonement'. The word means 'at-one-ment', or reconciliation with God. In ancient times the High Priest in the temple would recite prayers over a goat and off-load the sins of the people on to it before sending it off into the wilderness. It is how the word 'scapegoat' originated. It celebrated the day Moses came down from Jebel Musa in Sinai bringing with him the second tablets of stone with God's commandments on them, marking God's forgiveness of his wayward people who, on Moses' first descent with the commandments, had been worshipping a golden calf.

Of course there were off-the-cuff explanations given for Israel's triumphant victory. Men always found reasons for success, and thank God for victory, rather than recognize the obvious facts that victory has been due to discipline, determination and superior military hardware. God hadn't been around to trigger miracles for his Jews when Rome, with its greater military capability, had destroyed the temple and thrown the Jews out of Jerusalem.

God's aid to the Moslems at the Battle of Badr, when three hundred of Muhammad's faithful had been miraculously mistaken for thousands, so striking terror into the hearts of the Meccan enemy, resulted in victory for Muḥammad, but had not been repeated at the Battle of Uhud when victory had gone to Muhammad's adversaries. The explanation for that first victory at the Battle of Badr was explained in the Koran: 'It was not you, but God, who slew them. It was not you who smote them: God smote them so that He might richly reward the faithful. God hears all and knows all. Even so; God will surely frustrate the designs of the unbelievers.' (Sura 8:17).

But had all the Syrians, Jordanians and Egyptians been categorized as 'unbelievers' when they'd been defeated in the Six Day War? Or had Muhammad and his Companions been 'unbelievers' when they'd lost the Battle of Uhud? In that battle Muhammad had been wounded and one of his best men had been killed. God decided to enlighten Muhammad with the reasons. It was because he and his followers had become over confident, were lacking in humility and not putting their entire faith in God. People can always give themselves a God answer if they believe. Take God out of the equation of life, though, and the answer lies in the reality of which army has the greatest strength, determination, and inspirational commanders with on-the-spur-of-the-moment decision-making abilities.

Michael pointed out a U.N. bus on a distant road. Only the U.N. was allowed to cross from Israel to Syria, he said. The Irish girl immediately wanted to know how long it would take to walk to the Syrian border. Michael eyed her silently for a moment, then said: "Forty-five minutes." He then added: "There are unexploded land mines out there," whereupon the Irish girl stared her two-second look, then closed her eyes for at least one minute as she digested this unwelcome bit of information, while Michael informed us that where we now stood was on a straight line as the crow flies from the Damascus Gate in Jerusalem to Damascus in Syria. When St. Paul had been going to Damascus, he said, he would have passed along where we were now standing.

To the west of us, the ridge of a hill bristled with technology and monitoring devices for tracking and recording and listening in on the enemy. Michael said I could take a photo which I did, but felt immediately a marked criminal, an enemy of God's beloved people. I feared that on our flight home I'd be stopped at the airport and taken into what was commonly known as 'administrative detention' where people were held indefinitely without trial.

As we drove back down from the Golan Heights my thoughts once more went back to Elias Chacour. As a young man he'd been offered a place at the Seminary of St. Sulpice in Paris to study theology. To his surprise he'd found there that his fellow French students believed the propaganda put around by Israelis that all Palestinians were terrorists. When Elias told them his own story about the destruction of his village, and the other humiliations endured by him and his family, they'd remarked that the Zionists obviously had to do whatever they could to protect themselves from terrorism; that they'd clearly had to clean out the villages before there could be peace.

Elias had controlled his indignation, and had quietly asked whether they really thought it right that a group of foreigners should forcefully crush a whole country full of powerless people and take over their land? All Palestinians were not fighters or terrorists, but rather it was they themselves, the Palestinians, who were being terrorized, he'd said.

During this period Elias Chacour received an invitation from an influential, wealthy Parisien to join him and his family and friends for Christmas at his country house. This had been Chacour's first Christmas away from Palestine, and he'd been feeling homesick so was grateful for the invitation. His host, however, who had confided to him earlier that he was to be his 'special guest from the Holy Land', had taken him around introducing him to everyone as his 'Jewish friend from Bethlehem'. Elias had quickly corrected this, but his host had been adamant, saying that it surely wasn't such a difficult thing for Elias to play the Jew from Bethlehem, rather than the Palestinian from a small village called Biram? And he'd gone on to tell him in no uncertain terms (a bit of fatherly advice) that he should realize by now that he'd get along much better if he'd just stop announcing to the world that he was Palestinian.

I was sad that it had been the British who'd been responsible for triggering this political disaster. In 1917 Balfour, the British foreign secretary, probably with one eye on the Bible, had started it all. He'd been the one to put before Rothschild (big money there), his famous Balfour Declaration in a private letter: 'His Majesty's Government views with favour the establishment in Palestine of a National Home for the Jewish people, and will use their best endeavours to facilitate the achievement of that object...'

From the coach Michael pointed out various Israeli landmarks as we drove down from the Golan Heights: a military camp, a monument to Israeli soldiers who'd fallen in battle, the River Jordan – I had hoped we'd stop by the Jordan as I'd have liked to have filled a small bottle with its water.

"Water from the Jordan – why on earth?" came the scathing remark from Harry when I told him.

I myself wondered why. Why, as a wavering atheist, would I want Jordan river water – just because John the Baptist had baptized people in it two thousand years ago? That was pathetic of me and sheer superstitious nonsense on my part.

"Probably polluted!" went on my beloved spouse. "You

won't be allowed to take it on the plane, and it will probably leak! Water from the river Jordan, ugh!"

Harry needn't have worried as Michael had no plan to stop. Instead the Canon read aloud from the first chapter of Mark's Gospel: 'John the baptizer appeared in the wilderness, preaching a baptism of repentance for the forgiveness of sins. And there went out to him all the country of Judaea, and all the people of Jerusalem; and they were baptized by him in the river Jordan, confessing their sins.'

I was quite interested because it seemed to me that this immersion of John's fellow Jews had been a customary Jewish ritual, the *mikveh,* an immersion in natural, flowing water, and a symbolic act of purification and rebirth into new beginnings. Proselytes, those who converted to the Jewish faith, had had to undergo this ritual as part of their conversion, and it had then been adopted by Christianity as a rite to be performed before acceptance into this new religion.

I was really curious about those who changed their faith. Why, if someone believed in God in one of the monotheistic religions, would he want to switch to another? People tended to say they'd been called by God to this or that. But, if they already had belief in God, why would he want to lead them into another faith which also believed in him?

The apostasy of the Emperor Julian (Julian the Apostate) was to me quite understandable because he'd wanted to return to the pagan gods of his ancestors. He'd been brought up a Christian but hadn't been able to understand the dogma. In fact, he had much more sympathy for the Jews as he equated their supreme God with the supreme Olympian Zeus. His dislike of Christianity and

Christians in general, prompted him to promise the Jews that he would rebuild their temple in Jerusalem.

But it was not to be. Julian led his army against the Persians and, with notable courage or maybe foolhardiness, he plunged himself into the thick of some battle without first strapping on his breastplate. His men, encouraged by his show of valiance, were pursuing the enemy when Julian was struck by a spear which proved fatal.

Legend has it that Julian before dying scooped a handful of blood from his wound and murmured: 'Thou hast conquered, Galilean!' A further legend is rumoured that the Virgin Mary miraculously resurrected a Christian army officer whom Julian had killed, a St. Mercurius, and it had been he who'd delivered the fatal wound to Julian. The legend goes on to claim that St. Basil had then had a dream instructing him to visit the tomb of St. Mercurius. There he'd found the blood-stained spear which had killed the emperor.

So Christian prayers were answered and Christianity triumphed at the expense of Judaism. I found it all very strange.

That night I wrote: *It is so ODD the Bible!*

Supposing it had never been written? Just supposing that! No one – just no one!! – could then get fanatical about its interpretation. There would be no Jews and, therefore, no Christians – just people. There would be no fundamentalists fulminating – there would have been no holocaust, no inquisition, no religious horrors.

If rabbis and priests and suchlike didn't put everything in the Bible down to the word of God, human beings might become perfectly sensible and behave reasonably, because it is more reasonable to behave that way and get along with others around you than not to.

Miracles? Prophecies? Divine vengeance? Not too sure about any of them. Miracles are surely, when all's said and done, only hopes fulfilled?

I really think everything's just chance, like Princess Di's death when everyone theorized about conspiracies because she was hobnobbing with Dodi. People found it impossible to accept that two cars could collide, boom! I suppose the mind/ imagination just has to seek out reasons for everything. A great earthquake on the Temple Mount at the time of Julian the Apostate's death was seen as a sign from God, though as likely as not it was just an earthquake caused by whatever causes them.

Too tired to think any more! Might think differently about everything tomorrow —

CHAPTER

10

CAPERNAUM
AND BANIAS

At Capernaum I tried not to feel saturated by an excess of Gospel quotes and Franciscan churches built on sites which fitted in with the life of Jesus as reported in the New Testament. We now stood beside the ruined walls of the house where Peter the disciple was reputed to have lived, and around which a modern sheets-of-glass octagonal church had been erected, looking rather like a capsule from outer space.

I tried to concentrate on the moment and to imagine Peter and his brother Andrew living there. They were both fishermen and had followed Jesus instantly when Jesus had seen them casting their nets into the Sea of Galilee, and had told them to leave everything to follow him.

Interestingly, in his *Hymn to Apollo*, Homer had written how those on board a ship bringing Apollo to Delphi had been told by Apollo to abandon their families on Crete and become his priests, which they had done without hesitation.

It is generally assumed that Jesus left Nazareth for Capernaum because his own family had become alarmed by his words and actions. Jesus is reported to have said: "'A prophet is not without honour except in his own country and in his own house."' (Matthew 13: 57). He was quite fierce about his family and on one occasion seemed even to have denied its very existence when he'd been told that his mother and brothers were outside and asking for him. He was reputed to have said: "'Who are my mother and my brothers?"' (Mark 3: 33). Quite baffling also were his words: "'If any one comes to me and does not hate his own father and mother and wife and children and brothers and sisters, yes, and even his own life, he cannot be my disciple...'" (Luke 14: 26).

What would the Canon say if I asked him about these passages? That the words really meant something else? That it was a bad translation?

"I love it here!" said the Irish girl having come out of her prayer mode back to the reality of the moment. "The Lord made Peter a fisher of men. Have you been to St. Peter's, Rome?" she enquired.

"No."

"It's grand there. But I like it here. It's nice to see where St. Peter lived before he was called."

"It's really strange how he grew in stature from such humble beginnings," I remarked.

"That is what belief in Our Lord does to people," she said. Then she added: "Holding the keys of the kingdom, that's how they show Peter. He knows the way. For those who want to follow, he will lead you to the kingdom."

We left Peter's house and followed Michael through the ruins. A few stunted palm trees grew amongst the excavations. The Sea of Galilee stretched away beyond the site. We were led to the Roman synagogue built over an earlier one believed to have been the synagogue where Jesus had preached. The synagogue was of grey-white limestone and looked somewhat similar to a small Roman temple but with stunted columns. There were Jewish symbols on some of the ornate capitals: the star of David, a menorah, pomegranates, palm leaves. Up on a limestone lintel was depicted a carriage carrying the Ark of the Covenant. The whole structure was sturdily elegant with stone seating running the length of the synagogue.

It was a place I would have liked to have sat in alone all afternoon, a place to ponder and wonder about the Almighty and the Bible. A place to put aside God's various images of being jealous, wrathful, or vengeful as described in the Jewish Old Testament, and consider the Son who was said by the disciples to preach love and peace but, nevertheless, was reported to have said the odd remark of having to hate your parents in order to gain the kingdom of heaven.

I remained divinely blinkered. I had no hope at all of understanding the incomprehensible. For example, it was here at Capernaum that St. John's Gospel recounts the extraordinary things Jesus said to the Jews: '"...unless you eat the flesh of the Son of man and drink his blood, you have no life in you... He who eats my flesh and drinks my blood abides in me, and I in him..."' (John 6: 53, 56).

It's not surprising after Jesus had said that St John wrote: 'many of his disciples drew back and no longer went about with him.' (John 6:66).

But where in the first place would Jesus have got the idea from? Apparently there were many pagans living in Galilee at that time. It was customary for the worshippers of Dionysos, god of wine, for instance, to tear bulls apart with their bare hands and eat the flesh while in an ecstatic trance. Bulls were symbolic of the god and in this way it was believed they received the power of Dionysos through the blood of the bull. Did Jesus know about this pagan rite?

As Jesus didn't begin his ministry till he was thirty, I could see no reason before then why he mightn't have 'lived a little', as they say. No reason why he mightn't have watched *The Bacchae,* a Greek tragedy by Euripides, which stresses the power of the god Dionysos. Why shouldn't Jesus have seen the play at, say, the amphitheatre at Caesarea? Or at Sepphoris which had earlier been the Roman administrative centre for Galilee and possessed a theatre? Its inhabitants had been Jews and Hellenists, and it was only three kilometres from Nazareth. Added to this, it is generally believed that the Virgin Mary's parents lived there which would have given Jesus a reason for frequent visits.

In *The Bacchae,* the Chorus stresses the power of the divine.Had Jesus seen a production of it and heard its opening line, it would have made him sit up and wonder at the sheer coincidence of it: 'Behold, God's Son is come unto this land...'

There'd been other miracle-workers and those claiming to be the Messiah before Jesus. Apparently Galilee at the time had been a breeding ground for holy men who'd been popular amongst ordinary people because they'd worked miracles. Several had had power over the winds and the rain. One such was thought to have been a reincarnation of Elijah. He was Hanina ben Dosa who'd lived around one hundred B.C. By prayer and the laying on of hands he'd been able to heal the sick. But neither he, nor any of the others, had claimed to be the Son of God. Jesus himself had been quite cagey about it – 'Son of man' had been the term he'd used most often, which always struck me as rather obvious. The explanation given to me by our local vicar (without any polite coughing first) was that it was a term used in the Old Testament for the Messiah. I immediately turned to a book by Geza Vermes, *The Authentic Gospel of Jesus,* where he explains at length this terminology and points out that it has no significance at all regarding Messiahship, but when taken back to its Jewish Aramaic meaning 'Son of man' is fairly inconsequential like saying 'yours truly'. The Gospel references to 'Son of man', he explains, is a deliberate ploy of the writers of the Gospels to 'create a degree of obscurity and inclusiveness' for Jesus.

I noticed the Canon sitting close by looking contentedly morose. I could have slid along the stone seat towards him to ask him to explain the unexplainable. But I remained where I was, not wanting to disturb his tranquillity.

I had already questioned him earlier that morning after we'd had a reading of the Beatitudes. The Scottish minister had read from the Gospel of St. Matthew at the Church of the Beatitudes. I'd been paying attention and hadn't been able to understand the meaning of 'Blessed are the poor in spirit, for theirs is the kingdom of heaven.' (Matthew 5: 3).

I'd seized my opportunity when I'd seen the Canon afterwards stalking along on his own as we'd been making our way back to the coach. He had looked down with his kindly, hangdog eyes as I'd come alongside him. I'd popped the question about the poor in spirit going to heaven. "What does it mean?" I'd asked. "Who are the 'poor in spirit'?"

The polite cough had indicated that his mind had been whirring into action looking for the answer. After about ten paces he'd said that he thought the Beatitudes needed to be looked at in the round, not sentence by sentence, and that I should read a book by some bishop who'd made a study of St. Matthew and there I would find the answer to my question.

Later when at home I ordered the book from the library and found it profoundly unhelpful. Perhaps I had the wrong book by the wrong bishop? Later still, however, I discovered quite by chance, the explanation given in Elias Chacour's second book, *We Belong to the Land*. Elias explained how it was all a matter of translation. He had learned Hebrew and English and Aramaic (besides other languages) and had himself been at odds with the English translation. The word 'Blessed' was the English given for the Greek New Testament word *'makarioi'* which itself was a translation of the Aramaic word *'ashray'* from the verb *'yashar'*. Aramaic was the language Jesus spoke. To quote from Elias Chacour's book: '...it means "to set yourself on the right way for the right goal; to turn around, repent; to become straight or righteous."' The word 'Blessed' was a very bad one if the true meaning of the Aramaic word *'ashray'* was to be conveyed, he wrote.

He went on: 'When I understand Jesus' words in the Aramaic, I translate like this:

"Get up, go ahead, do something, move, you who are hungry and thirsty for justice, for you shall be satisfied.

"Get up, go ahead, do something, move, you peacemakers, for you shall be called children of God."'

That was fascinating. So now I had to read the first line of the Beatitudes as: 'Get up, go ahead, do something, move, you poor in spirit, for you shall have the kingdom of God'. It made me wonder what else was badly translated.

Sitting there on the stone seat in the Capernaum synagogue I was very tempted to put another question to the Canon. But I really didn't like to disturb him. Why, I wanted to know, when Jesus appeared to his disciples after his death had he never been immediately recognized? As I'd remarked to Harry when we'd been at the Church of Peter's Primacy beside the Sea of Galilee, he'd been seen as just a stranger on the shore when Peter and John and several other apostles had been fishing and had caught nothing all night. Jesus had called out to them to cast their net on the other side of the boat, whereupon they'd caught such a quantity they'd been unable to haul it in. When they'd come ashore there had been a charcoal fire and Jesus (still unrecognized) had invited them to breakfast. A rock inside the church known today as *Mensa Christi* (Jesus' table) is where tradition has it they ate together.

"Why do you suppose he was unrecognized?" I'd asked Harry.

"Well, I suppose he was a spirit," Harry had suggested vaguely.

"Well, Mary Magdalene, when she saw him outside his tomb in Jerusalem, thought he was the gardener," I'd remarked. "If you'd died and I saw an apparition, and it was you come back, then it'd be only sensible for you to look like you, not the gardener. And if you're going to say that Jesus wasn't an apparition but the risen Lord, all the more reason to look like himself and not a stranger."

Sitting quietly here at Capernaum I wondered suddenly whether Jesus hadn't been recognized because he'd been a non-person. A Son of God might well have gone about as nothing more than a 'Word' or an 'idea' in the first place. After all, early Christians had said that the pagan gods had been 'ideas' or 'words'. If God existed and wanted to put knowledge of himself about amongst the Gentiles, then how better to do it than by planting the 'Word' in the minds of men? 'In the beginning was the Word' (John 1: 1) It sort of made sense. Or maybe not. It occurred to me then that nowhere in any of the Gospels was there a description of what Jesus had looked like. Only artists had depicted him as tall and slim with long dark hair.

The elderly Scottish woman approached me. "Oooh, pet," she said gently, "I think I'll take the weight off my feet whilst we've a wee moment." She sat down and stretched her legs out in front of her. I could see the swollen ankles bulging over her canvas shoes.

"They must be painful," I said, indicating her feet.

"Aye, they are that. But they've time enough to get better when I'm back home," she said uncomplainingly. "You can't expect miracles at my age. And what about you, pet? Are you enjoying your time out here?"

"Fascinating," I replied. "I shall always remember this morning down by the Sea of Galilee."

Not far from the Church of Peter's Primacy, we'd been taken through an area of trees and flowering shrubs, past a fast flowing stream, down to an isolated spot beside the Sea of Galilee. On the shore there had been a thatched shelter, wooden benches and a big oblong rock which served as an altar, with the glittering sheen of the Sea of Galilee a few feet away. There had been a cross and a chalice on the altar which were silhouettes against the blue sky. A bird, maybe a crane, had flown low over the sea.

I showed her a heavily veined burnished gold leaf I had picked up from the area. I had taken it as a memento of the occasion. The tranquillity had been so absolute in that particular location that I hadn't rebelled but had dutifully taken the sacraments, even though I hadn't felt repentant, hadn't felt meek and didn't believe. It had been a marvellously isolated spot which had to be booked in advance by group leaders so that Holy Communions could be celebrated there without disturbance. Apart from the thatched shelter there had been several trees offering shade. Beyond us along the shore had been a few palm trees. The Sea of Galilee had been smooth as a mirror, making soft lapping sounds on the sandy shingle. Across the water the Golan Heights had loomed through the haze.

I saw that Michael was summoning us. The next stop would be Banias.

Michael informed us that Banias was the Caesarea Philippi of the New Testament. It was known as Banias under the Hellenists and Romans, and it had been Herod the Great who'd built a temple here in honour of Caesar Augustus. Later, his son Philip had enlarged the town, and had renamed it Caesarea Philippi after himself. Michael went on to tell us that it was originally called Banias after Pan, the Greek god who was half man, half goat. Pan combined with the Greek word 'gaea' pronounced 'yaea' ('earth') was 'Pan-yaea' and, as the Arabs had no 'P' in their alphabet, so it had become Banias.

I wondered why the Greek god Pan had received such honour at this place. He'd had no significant sacred site in Greece, and had merely been a minor deity-come-goat figure who was said to dance about wild mountainous terrain on cloven hooves playing his Pan pipes – a sort of enchanting idea belonging to the hills of Arcadia than to anywhere else.

Banias was unusually lush with streams and waterfalls, leafy trees and contrastingly barren lofty rocky escarpments. Here and there in the rockface were recesses where statues of Pan and his nymphs had once stood. A marble terrace with white marble ruins stretched along the base of the escarpment; these were all that remained of Herod the Great's temple of Caesar Augustus.

We stood in the midday sun as the Canon read from Matthew 16: 13-20.

'Now when Jesus came into the district of Caesarea Philippi, he asked his disciples, "Who do men say that the Son of man is?" And they said, "Some say John the Baptist, others say Elijah, and others Jeremiah or one of the prophets." He said to them, "But who do you say that I am?" Simon Peter replied, "You are the Christ, the Son of the living God." And Jesus answered him, "Blessed are you Simon Bar-Jona! For flesh and blood has not revealed this to you, but my Father who is in heaven. And I tell you, you are Peter, and on this rock I will build my church, and the powers of death shall not prevail against it. I will give you the keys of the kingdom of heaven, and whatever you bind on earth shall be bound in heaven, and whatever you loose on earth shall be loosed in heaven." Then he strictly charged the disciples to tell no one that he was the Christ.' With a thoughtful expression the Canon closed his New Testament.

When later at home I discovered Elias Chacour's interpretation of 'Blessed' in the Beatitudes, I tried to unravel the Greek New Testament regarding the same passage which the Canon had just read. My translation of the Greek made the 'Son of the living God' into 'Son of the God of life' which was really rather different.

As for the passage '...and the powers of death shall not prevail against it (my church)...', I thought it should really be 'the portals of Hades shall not prevail...' That was fascinating as Hades was the Greek god of the underworld. There was something slightly suspicious about leaving the translation of the Greek New Testament to avowed Christians who only translated it according to their convictions. For instance, '...on this rock I will build my church...' the word church is surely an anachronism as there was no church at the time of Jesus and anyway the word in the Greek New Testament is 'ekklesia' which originally meant 'a gathering of citizens'. It was odd how words could change meaning over the centuries.

But worst of all, I thought the passage 'I will give you the keys of the kingdom' should read 'keys of the queen of the heavens' – well! As Harry said when I came up with this exciting bit of information, it was obviously time for me to stop meddling in Greek texts if I couldn't make a better job of it.

While at Caesarea Philippi, however, I was happily ignorant regarding translations and more absorbed in the immediate surroundings of barren rock, white marble ruins, streams and different hues of green foliage.

"What are you thinking?" the Irish girl enquired, approaching me purposefully.

"Well, I was wondering whether Jesus knew about the god Pan," I said.

"Why would Our Lord know that?" she demanded.

"Well, why shouldn't he?" I asked. "He couldn't have been unaware of Pan, or the temple of Caesar Augustus?" I ventured.

"Our Lord was only interested in doing his Father's business on earth," she said.

"But he surely couldn't have been blind to other religions around him?" I queried.

"I only believe what the Gospels tell us. Anything else is rubbish!" she declared, and left me abruptly, clutching her shoulder-bag under her arm.

I found Harry and we wandered along a track with the

barren rockface on our right and lush greenery and streams to our left. But we had only twenty minutes before we were expected back at the coach.

We sat on a wooden seat and stared down into the green foliage of trees and shrubs below us.

"I wonder what Jesus really knew about the gods of the gentiles?" I remarked.

"Why would he know anything?" came the prompt response.

"Well, I'd have thought some of the gentile beliefs must have rubbed off on him. And if not on Jesus in particular then on some of his disciples or, at any rate, on those who wrote the Gospels. This was gentile territory at the time of Christ, so 'Son of God' would have been natural – well, at least understood by Greeks and Romans. Peter saying to Jesus he was the Son of God wouldn't have been so amazing."

"I thought Jesus was fulfilling prophecy as the Messiah?" said Harry with conviction, asking it as a question.

"Well, that's what the Gospel writers wanted to establish. But the very fact that nothing was recorded at the time of Jesus but only several decades after his death, is quite incredibly peculiar. Anyway, I'm only wondering how much Jesus knew about Greek and Roman culture. I mean, did he sing or dance or go to the theatre, or attend sporting events? Or was he married to Mary Magdalene as the *Da Vinci Code* book claims? In which case did God have grandchildren?"

"Have you quite finished?"

"I think I've only just begun."

Harry closed his eyes against the sun's rays. "Just ask the Canon if you want to know anything. You might as well take advantage of travelling with one!" was his sober advice.

★

That night I scribbled:

I'm annoyed with myself! I've been so taken up with seeing places as reported in the Bible, that I completely forgot to look out for places linked to St. George! To forget what I wanted to remember! Ridiculous!

Why did I want to remember him? Because St. George is the patron saint of England AND, believe it or not, of Palestine. The Moslems call him Al-Khader and have great faith in him as a miracle-worker. They believe he flies through the air in split seconds. At Banias somewhere (didn't see or look, because I'd forgotten) there's a domed shrine sacred to him.

Also, close to Bethlehem there's a village called Al-Khader in which there is a Church of St. George run by the Greek Orthodox Church. Moslems come to it with equal reverence as Christians, and even baptize their children in the font in the name of St. George, believing this will make them strong. Interesting! Any child with some nervous/mental disorder will be brought by his parents to the Greek Orthodox priest hoping for a miracle. For instance, a mute child will have a key inserted in his mouth by the priest, and in the name of St. George will symbolically unlock the problem. Moslems come to the church with their own prayer-mats and pray towards the icon of St. George which is placed on a wall so that they face Mecca.

St. George or Al-Khader was said to have been born in Cappadocia. He died a martyr's death and was buried at Lydda (called Lod today) which is close to the Ben Gurion International airport where we arrived. Pity we can't do a quick sprint to it before we leave. There are big celebrations there on St. George's day. Now I think of it Al-Khader also has a shrine in the Dome of the Rock.

His slaying of a dragon image I always think is an echo

of Apollo slaying the dragon/python at Delphi. The village of Aráchova a few miles from Delphi has a three-day festival in which a number of things concerning St. George reflect legends of Apollo.

The Crusaders were very taken with St. George when they came to the Holy Land because he was a soldier saint. He didn't officially become patron saint of England till mid-fourteenth century. Am I right in thinking that the Crusaders had a banner of a red cross on a white background which is St. George's flag? Don't know which came first though, St. George's flag or the Crusader banner, so have to cough politely like the Canon when he can't answer a question.

It's odd really. The Canon's polite cough comes after years of experience. It takes three or four years training before ordination, yet all that priests seem to do when asked something controversial is to cough. Really! Must cut loose from religion altogether and just enjoy total freedom from it. Only sure of me! I can ask myself questions and be certain of an honest answer according to what I think, not what I OUGHT to think, or what others think.

Midges coming in, must turn off the light. More tomorrow.

CHAPTER

11

TIBERIAS AND
THE SEA OF GALILEE

It was mid-morning and we were on a 'Jesus Boat', a large wooden vessel with an awning. A couple of swarthies were manning it, and an Israeli flag fluttered from the mast-head. We were sailing north and the last few houses of Tiberias had just slipped from view. We were told that soon the black basalt Church of Peter's Primacy beside the shore would come into view. There was a disappointing and annoying haze, and the sky was what I could only call a non-colour; the Sea of Galilee itself was grey-blue merging to silver at its horizon.

Early that morning I had sat out on the terrace of our hotel and had watched as the tip of the sun had appeared above the Golan Heights, an orange-red disk; at that time the hills had been sharply delineated and clearly visible. After a few minutes, when the sun had risen higher, it had become a shining white pearl suffusing the sky in a sheen of mother-of-pearl light which in turn cast a misty grey haze like a gauze veil across the Golan Heights. It was strange this quick change in light and visibility.

Yesterday evening, while we'd been relaxing on the

terrace, a lone Jesus Boat had passed way offshore and a tenor voice had drifted clearly across the water singing a dreamy repetitive refrain: 'Aaa-a-li-luuu-yia... Aaa-a-li-luyia. Aaa-a-li-luuu-yia... Aaa-a-li-luyia'. The voice had had an eloquent beauty to it. The only other sound had been the gentle lapping of wavelets, and the soughing of palm fronds as a light breeze caught them. Three cormorants had skimmed the water, heading for wherever cormorants fly in the evening.

Later that night the Irish girl had confided her latest escapade. She had been walking through Tiberias when a young man had tapped her on the shoulder from behind. He had wanted her to go back with him to his hotel where he was employed as a waiter. He had then informed her that he was an Israeli citizen from Australia doing his national service. But, she asked me, didn't I think it odd that he should say that? How could he be doing his national service if he was working as a waiter in a hotel? And didn't I think it wrong of him to ask her back to his hotel where he was working? What did I think? I'd said that I thought young female tourists were regarded as fair game abroad. "Oh, do you think so?" she'd asked, her eyes more closed than open but with a distinct sparkle to them. "So you think it's sexual?" she'd queried. "Well, what do you think?" I'd asked. "He said he was twenty-seven. He couldn't be doing his national service, not if he was a waiter. Shall I visit him in his hotel? What do you think?" I'd replied that she shouldn't get herself into a situation she'd regret. But if she didn't think she'd regret it, then to go ahead. The subject had ended there and, after supper, I'd seen 'Gorgeous' at the reception desk, but the Irish girl was nowhere to be seen. I could only guess where she'd gone.

The engine of the Jesus Boat we were on, cut out and

we drifted in silence. The Canon wanted us to experience the tranquillity of the Sea of Galilee. After a minute or two he stood up and read the passage from Matthew 14: 22-33 about the disciples battling against the wind far out on the Sea of Galilee and, when all seemed against them, seeing Jesus walking on the water towards them which had terrified them as they thought they'd seen a ghost. Peter had then said to Jesus that if he was really walking on the sea then he could do it too. Whereupon he got out of the boat and walked towards Jesus. But when he saw the wind, he began to sink – not that wind can be seen, only waves whipped up by it – but the message that supreme faith was needed was clear.

The Sea of Galilee was very much part of the Gospel stories. On one occasion Jesus took himself off alone in a boat when he learned that his relative, John the Baptist, had been beheaded. He believed that John the Baptist was Elijah and heralded his own coming as the Messiah – that Elijah would precede the Messiah was a common Jewish expectation.

I said as much to Harry. "It must have been a profound shock to believe you are the Messiah and find your expectations disintegrating around you," I began. "I mean, to hear that your forerunner has been beheaded! Can you imagine the shock? So you go off in a boat to come to terms with the new situation that you're not, perhaps, the Messiah after all. Then again you get a sort of inkling that you are because you go up a mountain and become transfigured with Moses and Elijah beside you, with a voice from a cloud telling you you are God's beloved Son."

"Are you speaking facts about the transfiguration or asking me questions about it?" Harry asked.

"I'm just pointing out how disturbing it must have been

for Jesus not being altogether sure but merely suspecting that he was."

"What makes you think he wasn't sure?"

"Well, from what I've read in the Gospels Jesus didn't sound at all convinced. It was the Christians afterwards who were adamant about it. Jesus kept telling his disciples to keep quiet about everything they saw and heard, which is a bit odd, I think."

"I shouldn't give it too much thought," the wise one said.

But I did give it more thought and pressed on: "I mean, if Elijah was thought to herald the coming of the Messiah, and John the Baptist was thought to be Elijah, then why didn't all the Jews recognize him as such? It must have been very difficult for Jesus keeping faith with himself with so many doubts in the air. It must have been too awful when John was beheaded. If, on the other hand, Jesus was just the 'Word' – just an 'Idea' – then that explains a lot, because he didn't really exist but Christians simply made Jesus what they wanted him to be: Messiah, Man and – " I felt a sharp poke and stopped abruptly. The Scottish minister was holding up his hand and was announcing the hymn *Eternal Father strong to save.* He beat the air vigorously as he gave voice: "Eternal Father strong to save..."

There was a young man with the Scottish group seated centrally under the awning. I had never seen him before, and for some reason began to suspect him of being a spy planted among us by the Israeli security forces. I was still absurdly anxious about the photograph I had taken of the Israeli military whatever-it-was on the Golan Heights the day before. In due course I learned that the young man was, in fact, the son of a couple on our pilgrimage and, far from being a spy, was working as a lawyer for the U.N. Human Rights Centre based in Haifa. I hoped very much to get an opportunity to question him about his work.

The boat's engine was restarted, and the W.I. woman began striding from one side of the boat to the other selecting new subjects for the slide show she was planning to give back home. She had already taken photos of the boat itself, the crew, the bows, the stern – "No can do, the shore's too far away," she declared, when someone pointed out the Church of Peter's Primacy. "I grant you this is the perfect opportunity to take everyone on the trip. Yes, while they're all sitting down! With any luck they won't even know I'm taking them. Get a better picture that way." With enthusiasm she pretended to be looking out across the water and, when her next quarry wasn't aware of it, she took a photo of him or her with exclamations: "Got her! Got you! Got him!"

The Irish girl left her place beside me and went and stood at the prow like a figurehead, her mop of curls streaming back from her face, her eyes only slits against the breeze. I wondered whose arms she was imagining were enfolding her – the handsome hotel receptionist helping her to read Arabic in Jerusalem, or the national service waiter here in Tiberias, or the 'Gorgeous' one at our hotel, or the camel dealer in Bethlehem?

My mind drifted to Josephus, the historian who'd written his *Jewish War* and had described the building of the port of Caesarea. He had been born in 37 A.D. and had become Governor of Galilee before he was thirty at the time of the first Jewish revolt – a very difficult position of authority to hold as he had also to keep the different Jewish factions from rebelling against each other. At one point he had nearly been killed in Tiberias by a Jewish mob but had managed to escape across the Sea of Galilee.

Later on Josephus had behaved quite appallingly

and had claimed it was the will of God he should turn traitor. He'd had a number of dreams which he'd divined as 'equivocal utterances of the Deity' and had sent up a 'secret prayer' (though not so secret that he didn't write about it in his book) saying: "'Inasmuch as it pleaseth Thee to visit Thy wrath on the Jewish people... I yield myself willingly to the Romans that I may live, but I solemnly declare that I go, not as a traitor, but as Thy servant.'"

How easily men can persuade themselves that God is guiding them.

The Canon's wife smiled sweetly and sat beside me where the Irish girl had been. She remarked that the boat trip had been a wonderful experience. To be on the Sea of Galilee seeing the same shoreline and landscape that had been seen by Our Lord and his disciples! To breathe in the same air! to be under the same sky! She sighed. "To think that from this small corner of Palestine a small spark set the world alight," she said with wonder. "Our Lord called his disciples, and through them came the new Christian religion – all part of Almighty God's divine plan for the world!" she murmured.

"It is remarkable how ideas get taken up and spread," I agreed dutifully.

"So much persecution and suffering came with it," she went on. "We're fortunate today that the Catholic Church no longer puts to death those who oppose its views."

"I wonder what the world would be like if there'd been no Christianity," I remarked.

"Oh, that doesn't bear thinking of!" she said, slightly hyper-ventillating at the thought. "There'd be no morality in the world. We can consider ourselves truly blessed to have our Christian values and all the other blessings that go with belief in Our Lord Jesus Christ." She fell silent, her face a flaming red from the heat, and perspiring slightly under her white sun-hat. Her blue eyes scanned the shoreline as the houses of Tiberias came back into view. "Yes, we are so lucky. So extremely fortunate," she repeated, as the engine to our Jesus Boat changed rhythm, and we slowly edged forward alongside the jetty beside our hotel. "Such a shame we fly home tomorrow," she said.

"A tomb? Why on earth do you want to see a tomb?" demanded Harry. We were basking on our hotel terrace.

"Well, its the tomb of an important rabbi," I replied.

"So?"

"Rabbi Akiva who in the second century believed he was the Messiah." (He actually never thought anything of the sort, and I'd got it wrong).

"So what?"

"Isn't it fascinating?"

Harry thought for a moment, then said: "No. What's fascinating about somebody who thought he was, but obviously wasn't?"

"Well, he was one of the leading scholars of his day, and was even said to have made a mystical journey to paradise and back. To think himself the Messiah I think is fascinating!"

"Meaning that those with less brain power and scholarship got it right with Jesus, is that what you mean?"

"The Jews didn't think Jesus was. And that's amazing."

Harry clearly wasn't going to move from his lounging position. I, on the other hand, knew that this was my only opportunity to visit this tomb which I had marked in my guide-book as a vital place of pilgrimage if the opportunity arose. If I didn't make the effort now I knew

I would always regret it. Somewhat reluctantly I sat up.

Harry remained inert but said: "You're not walking there, not on your own."

"I'll get a taxi to collect me from here," I replied.

"God! what a waste of money! But don't let me stop you!" He opened one eye, saw that nothing he could say would make me back down, so closed the eye again with a resigned grunt.

The taxi-driver was a heavily built, dark-haired Jew of about forty with thick curly eyelashes. I sat beside him and thought it a good opportunity to enquire about life in Israel from a Jewish point of view. I asked him if he came from Tiberias. Yes, he was born here. Married? Yes, he was married and had two children. I kept up the prattle. Had he done his national service? Yes, yes.

"So where did you do it?" I enquired.

For some reason he didn't answer but picked up his mobile and let fly in Hebrew to a voice which sounded as if it was breaking through from outer space.

When he stopped speaking, I asked my question again. But there was another phone interruption and he again ignored me. Whereupon what seemed like a dozen squeals and bleeps, and voices breaking through stratas of atmosphere clamoured for his attention. I wondered if I was being taken hostage and these were his accomplices hiding out on the Golan Heights. I'd no idea where the tomb was but had read it was in Tiberias and easily reached. Instead, we seemed to be driving for ever and heading out of the city. I realized with dismay that I couldn't remember the name of my hotel. I only knew vaguely that its location was somewhere by the Sea of Galilee going north. Um. On the other hand, since he'd picked me up he must know where to put me down.

"How far?" I asked meekly when there was a brief silence.

"Soon. Very soon. Me, good guide. Speak good English."

"Yes, very good English. Have you been to England?"

"Yes, yes. England. Rain. London. I see bug in ham – " He paused and I was about to apologize for the weather and the food, but he went on: "Paliss. Bug in ham Paliss and Truffle Gars-queer. That I see." He looked down at me through his curly lashes and pointed to himself. "I – I speak four language good."

Did he just!

I really wanted some feedback on Israel from a Jewish standpoint. "So where were you in the army?" I enquired for the third time. It was as if the question set off fire alarms, because yet again the mobile rang and voices squawked.

He was still barking questions, or giving orders in short commanding bursts, when he drew up alongside blue painted railings surrounding something like a black-roofed Nissen hut.

"Tombi," he said to me. "Rabbi Akiva tombi."

We were beside a sort of stony wasteland, with a view over Tiberias to the Sea of Galilee which looked a shimmering deep blue in the hot midday sun.

Apart from two men chatting outside a wooden booth, there was only a solitary Orthodox Jew in a sort of whitewashed area, the walls of which were lined with bookshelves. He had dangling side curls, and was wearing a black hat and a long black coat despite the heat, and was seated at a table with an open book before him. He didn't raise his head on my arrival, but continued his studies, rocking backwards and forwards in concentration.

I went down some concrete steps to the Nissen-hut

type tomb and walked around it. There was Hebrew written on it. I had to admit that Harry was right when he'd said it was a complete waste of money, but how was I to know that without having made the effort to see for myself.

What I never admitted to Harry, which was something I didn't discover till we were back in England, was that Rabbi Akiva didn't think that he himself was the Messiah, but thought the commander who had led the second Jewish revolt against the Romans was.

The second Jewish revolt had lasted three years, from 132-135 A.D., and the commander had been Simeon Bar Koziba. He was the one who had used the appellation *Bar Kokhba,* the Messianic title meaning 'Son of a Star'. He'd also taken the title *Nasi* which could only be used by someone descended from the House of David – could *Nasi* be another explanation for Nazareth (Nasi-reth)?

To all extents and purposes this fierce guerilla fighter had had all the Jewish Messiahship credentials (and, no doubt, he himself thought he was the Messiah). So it hadn't been unreasonable for Rabbi Akiva to get excited about the thought that ancient Old Testament prophecy was at last being fulfilled, especially in opposition to what the Christian faith had been claiming for Jesus who'd been a pacifist. Rabbi Akiva's hopes and belief that Bar Koziba was the long awaited Messiah must have seemed confirmed when Bar Koziba captured Jerusalem from the Romans and managed to hold out there for three whole years – a quite remarkable feat of endurance.

Rome, however, had no intention of being made a fool of in this manner, and this second Jewish revolt had ended in tears when in 135 A.D. Jerusalem fell to the Romans once more and Bar Koziba and his men were killed. Poor Rabbi Akiva's world of scholarship and wisdom must have blown apart with the death of his 'Messiah'. Even so, he himself had lived on till he was a hundred and twenty when he'd been tortured to death under the Emperor Hadrian's persecution of the Jews. Despite dying in agony, Rabbi Akiva had, nevertheless, managed to die smiling and praising God.

Rabbi Akiva had been born in 50 A.D. so he would have been well advanced in years when he'd regarded Simeon Bar Koziba as the long awaited Messiah. But what, I wondered, had he thought about Jesus whom the Christians (those early Jews) had declared to be the Messiah?

While standing before the tomb of Rabbi Akiva, and feeling something of a fool being there at all, I suddenly wondered whether the whole 'Jesus was the Messiah' idea might have been a calculated Roman plot to teach the Jews a lesson for having been such a thorn in the flesh to them. Supposing they'd set up Roman guards in front of the sepulchre where Jesus's crucified body had been laid and, in the night they'd rolled back the stone and stolen the body?

I supposed that didn't explain the sightings. But, then the seeing of the risen Jesus hadn't been written about until thirty or forty years after his death – and had never been mentioned in Jewish scripture. By that time the Roman idea of a dying and risen deity – such as Dionysos who rose annually from the dead – could have worked itself into the minds of susceptible Jews or gentiles looking for signs and wonders. The New Testament had been written in Greek, so Greek minds would have put their stamp on things according to Greek ideas of gods, deaths and risings?

I could imagine the plot being hatched: 'We are the victorious Romans! Let's spin a miracle worker and make him the Messiah! In this way we'll divide the Jews into ever more factions. We'll spin the tale and leak it to the world in gospels, the 'good news', and give this Jesus traits of our god Bacchus (the Greek Dionysos). Yes! that's what we'll do! AND!!! we'll use Paul to get it all started with a blinding light!!'

Thinking these Messianic thoughts in the presence of Rabbi Akiva's tomb, and feeling a complete dolt for being there at all, I returned to my taxi-driver, and compounded my idiocy by asking to be taken on to the tomb of the great Jewish philospher and sage, Maimonides, which I had also marked in my guide-book as a place to visit if given the opportunity.

Maimonides was a twelfth century Spanish Jew, a philosopher, whose parents fled to Egypt from persecution in Spain. There he became physician to Saladin in Cairo. After completing scholarly research concerning the *Mishnah*, Maimonides wrote an important philosophical work called *Guide for the Perplexed* which was something from which every perplexed person could seek enlightenment. In it Maimonides tried to link reason and scripture, science and religion. I'd started to read an abridged version and was delighted and enraptured by his kindly disposition, and step by step explanations to the dim-witted – why this, and why that. But, after a number of pages, I'd got bored, preferring to remain perplexed than to continue with his exegesis which told me what and how I should be thinking.

We drove a shortish distance, then drew up in a large parking area beside a couple of domed buildings. "Tombi Maimonides," said my taxi-driver. Oriental music blared, and dozens of families were circulating in a nearby courtyard. A lamb was being barbecued, and the sound of ululating could be heard above the strident music.

I felt uncomfortably conspicuous as a lone English woman venturing into the crowds. I was glaringly not part of any family there. I made my way through the throng, and wanted very much to ask questions but nobody looked in my direction; all appeared engrossed in their family gatherings. I suspected that the people there were attending memorials for their deceased.

Maimonides had told his students that when he died his body was to be put on a camel and his final resting place was to be wherever the camel ended up. Maybe Maimonides believed, as Muhammad had, that his camel, Qaswa, was receptive to the will of Allah. Qaswa had, for instance, lain down and refused to budge on Muhammad's arrival at Medina when he had fled from Mecca. This, Muhammad had decided, was clearly where Allah intended he should live and build a mosque. Qaswa had also stubbornly refused to carry him to Mecca for the first Moslem hajj, and all the shoutings and beatings hadn't persuaded Qaswa to move, whereupon Muhammad had taken it as a sign from Allah that the time was not yet right for this new Moslem pilgrimage.

Whether it was Allah's will or not, Maimonides' camel had plodded on bearing his corpse until it reached Tiberias. Maybe the sniff of the waters of the Sea of Galilee enticed it. Here must have been where the camel stopped with the body of Maimonides.

Battered mentally by the crowds, the blaring music and ululating women, I returned to my taxi-driver and asked to be taken back to my hotel. Fortunately, he knew where to go. I tried one last attempt to sound him out about his time in the Israeli army, only to be thwarted by the mobile phone ringing and more squealing and squawking voices. I began to think the taxi must be wired up to some sort of secret service Israeli listening-in device. Well, let them listen! I was getting no interesting information from this man.

Harry was still lounging when I got back to the hotel.

"Sorted out the Messiahs?" he enquired, putting down the hotel's Bible he had found beside his bed.

"It was interesting," I said guardedly, not wanting to tell him how much the taxi-driver had charged, or my disappointment with Rabbi Akiva's tomb nor, for that matter, my unnecessary visit to the tomb of Maimonides.

"I've been reading St. Luke's version of Christ's trial," Harry remarked.

"Really?" I was surprised as I had never in my life seen Harry read the Bible.

"I was wondering why Herod and his soldiers treated Jesus with contempt. I suppose they were afraid the Romans would come down like a ton of bricks on them if they weren't severe with Jesus. Though I can't see that he was exactly doing anything particularly wrong."

"If he existed at all," I said, giving vent to my Roman plot thoughts.

Apparently, despite being questioned 'at some length' by Herod Antipas, Jesus had remained silent while the 'chief priests and the scribes stood by, vehemently accusing him'. St. Luke's Gospel tells us how Herod finally sent Jesus back to Pilate arrayed in 'gorgeous apparel', and Herod and Pilate had inexplicably then become good friends, having formerly been enemies. (Luke 23: 11, 12). The strange thing being that not once did Jesus defend himself, having been questioned and given every chance to say he was the Son of God, the Messiah, the Saviour of the world, Redeemer, or any of the numerous epithets which have since become attached to his name.

"Do you suppose the Gospels were written as deliberate anti-Semitic writings?" I suggested, trying Harry with my Roman plot thought.

"Hum."

"I mean the Jews were such thorns in the flesh of the Romans that the Gospel writers could have been paid by them to concoct a damn-the-Jews fiction which somehow backfired on the Romans, snuffing out their old gods and becoming another religion instead?"

"I don't think that can be so," came the sober response.

Another relevant idea had occurred to me since first considering this plot theory. Jesus, according to the Gospels, had been betrayed by Judas. Was it sheer coincidence that the name Judas was the Greek for Judah? In other words the betrayer of Jesus represented the Kingdom of Judah, the Jews?

I put the thought to Harry. "Don't ask me, ask the Canon," came the instant answer. And he put down the Bible, and closed his eyes to show that the subject was closed.

The champagne corks popped and shot so high that they hit an upstairs window of our hotel. An olive-faced Chinaman peered with alarm from the door to his balcony, opening it just wide enough to survey the scene. General laughter and good-humoured remarks reassured him that all was well. He shrugged and gave a dismissive wave before withdrawing and closing the door after him.

The couple whose son worked for the United Nations Human Rights Centre in Haifa, the one I had taken for a spy on the Jesus Boat, was giving a party. The occasion was to mark both the end of this trip, and also to celebrate the renewal of marriage vows taken by the couple several days earlier at Cana. The short service had been conducted by the Scottish minister in the church built where Jesus had performed his first miracle when turning water into wine at a wedding feast. Interestingly, Dionysos (god of wine and drama, and son of Olympian Zeus) was also said to have turned water into wine.

"Pagan gods were only imaginary figures with human characteristics," Harry had remarked when I'd told him this regarding Dionysos.

"You mean they are gods in Man's image?" I'd suggested.

"I suppose so."

"So Jesus could have been another god in Man's image but with a Jewish background which linked him to the Almighty?"

"You could say that," had been the unexpected reply.

"When all is said and done, all can be achieved in the human imagination," I'd added with aplomb.

"Well, I'm sure you're right," had been Harry's vague response.

In Cana the Scottish minister had asked if we would also like to renew our marriage vows, and Harry had immediately said he'd rather not. I wasn't sure how to take this. Harry must have realized he could have put it better because he'd explained later that since we'd already taken our vows, there was absolutely no need to take the wretched vows again. I must have continued looking somewhat disconcerted, because he'd finally said that a vow was a vow, and to keep having to vow was ridiculous. He'd then taken my hand and given it a reassuring pat.

We'd watched the Irish couple going through the

ceremony, and the husband being told at the end that he could kiss his bride which he'd dutifully done. Harry and I would have found it all very cringing had we been the centre of such attention. As observers of another couple renewing their vows, however, it had really been quite touching.

At this party now I saw Michael standing alone and looking somewhat out of things. For once he wasn't playing the role of guide but of guest. I smiled and went up to him and told him of my visit to Rabbi Akiva's tomb. He looked surprised that I had gone there.

"Did you visit the tomb of Maimonides?" he asked.

"Yes, I did," I replied. I asked Michael why there'd been so many family celebrations there, and he said they would have been holding bar mitzvahs.

"Not family memorials?" I enquired.

"Maybe those too," he said, giving me one of his rare mischievous smiles, and looking at me with his sexy brown eyes. Perhaps Harry should have insisted we renew our marriage vows –

"Your English, where did you learn it?" I asked.

"In England," he replied.

"In England?" It was more of an amazed exclamation than a question.

"I was educated in England and grew up in Sussex."

"That's why you come out with English idioms like 'it's not my cup of tea', or 'sailing too close to the wind'," I remarked.

The Irish girl came up, a purposeful look in her eyes. "I'd like to ask you a question about Nazareth," she began. Michael put on his guide's guarded expression as he braced himself for what might be an Irish girl flirtation disguised as a serious consultation. I noticed the Canon nearby talking to the Irish couple's son, then making his excuses as his wife drew him away.

This was my opportunity to speak to the young man. I left Michael with the Irish girl, introduced myself and leapt with both feet straight into the quagmire of Israeli/ Palestinian religious and political controversy.

"How can they grab land, bulldoze Palestinian villages and build their so-called 'defence' wall and expect peace?" I demanded.

The young lawyer, who must have heard it repeatedly whenever he announced he worked for human rights in Israel, remained calm and unruffled. He had learned the wisdom of silence as others let fly with their pro- or anti-Zionist opinions. I mentioned the despair of the head-master of the school in Nazareth, and the faith of Alice Sahhar at her Palestinian orphanage in Bethany, and also of X and his thwarted dreams of opening a restaurant in Bethlehem. Instead of keeping my promise to Harry of remaining uncontroversial regarding religion, I blurted out: "How can these Palestinian Christians go on believing that all will eventually come right through continuous prayer and faith in God?"

He continued to eye me calmly.

"You wouldn't advocate violence, would you?" he asked quietly.

I turned his question around. "The Israelis must be absolutely delighted with those Palestinians who are adopting this praying, Gandhi-like, peaceful-do-nothing policy," I countered. "So long as those who have this non-violence-against-the-Israelis campaign then they, the Israelis, can go on grabbing, bulldozing, imprisoning and torturing."

He smiled an enigmatic Mona Lisa sort of patient-know-it-all smile, as I continued firing missiles of opinions and lobbing grenades of explosive material at him. "And it's all our fault, that's what makes me so upset," I said. He looked puzzled. "The fault of Britain," I explained.

"Would you like it to return to pre-British Mandate days, to a purely Arab Palestine?" asked my human rights hostage whose ear I had.

"Jews and Palestinians lived perfectly happily side by side pre-war," I remarked.

"So what are you suggesting? What would your solution be?" he challenged.

I had the solution, and let it fly. "If only Jews wouldn't go on and on about their Jewishness, and keep pointing to Scripture as holding the key to everything, there wouldn't be all this trouble," I declared.

He eyed me warily. "I take it you're not anti-Semitic?"

"Not at all. But I am anti-Bible," I found myself saying. As he seemed to wait for me to continue, I continued: "It seems to me that all the troubles today stem from over-belief in things that were written millenia ago. It's appalling the way politicians have to grovel to Old Testament Bible thumpers in order to win Jewish votes to get into power!"

"I take your point," said the young man.

"So the only answer is to scrap the Bible," I said, crashing irredeemably through the take-care-what-you-say barrier.

"But you're surely not an atheist?" asked the young man, looking mildly anxious.

"Well, look at what's been achieved in the name of God!" I exploded. The young man raised an eyebrow. "Suspicion, misery, genocide in one form or another. It's too awful what people have done believing that their compulsive urges are God's guiding hand. To answer your question, I'm not a believer in the supremacy of the Jewish God, but I do believe in the eternal supremacy of a holy spirit."

"Isn't the Holy Spirit God? How can you believe in the one without the other?" came the enquiry.

"The Holy Spirit has never written Scripture! Never promised a land to a tribe of people and taught them a lot of nonsense which has turned them into land grabbers."

"I think you'll find a lot of Israelis today are, in fact, secular. Many don't believe in God or things written."

"Oh, then that just makes it worse!"

"Worse?"

"To go and grab Palestinian land with the justification that they are God's chosen and it's all in the Bible, and then to say that many don't believe in God at all, makes it a thousand times worse!"

The Scottish minister marched up to us and I had at once to tone down my outpourings. All I said was: "Can anything be done at all to right the obvious wrongs?"

"Things can only change through diplomacy and pressure groups," he remarked. "You could join Amnesty International if you feel you want to help," he remarked.

"If the Israelis won't obey U.N. resolutions, you won't find them listening to Amnesty International," said the ex-soldier. "Your mother has sent me over to convey a short message. She wants you to open another bottle of the bubbly. See how high you can pop the cork this time!"

That night I scribbled: *It's no good getting buoyed up and militant about things out here! I can't do anything about God and his Jews, their beliefs or their non-beliefs.*

I can do something about Alice Sahhar and her orphanage, though. In fact, I must do something and not just let her and her work slide away into oblivion once I get home.

Maybe I can give talks about the orphanage and raise money for it? I've never spoken in public in my life! But there's no reason not to – after all, I have a voice and can speak!

I talked to the W.I. woman at the party, and out of the blue she suddenly confided in me a long-held secret. She was widowed about five years ago, her husband having died of cancer after a long illness. She told me how one night a few days before his death she'd been trying to sleep and she'd told him to call her if he needed anything. After about half an hour she'd heard him call and, because of her extreme exhaustion, she'd pretended not to hear. He hadn't called again. Her story is incredibly sad. Quite incredibly awful and sad. How is it that life can hold such fun and laughter as well as the extreme opposite – abject misery. The W.I. woman and I were seated on a low wall and she'd given a 'Ha, ha, ha,' sort of laugh and said: "By golly! and I've never told a soul before! It must be the champagne!" She was then as cheerful and full of zest for all we'd done and were doing as she'd ever been, and soon her buddies had gathered round to talk about getting packed and ready for the journey home. I now look on her with wonder and admiration. She's been through hell but has, like someone on the point of drowning, managed to bob up to the surface, get back to land and regain her natural equilibrium and exuberance.

That the Christian Church is there to envelop all human needs is, I suppose, a good thing. For those who are church-goers it sustains them. For those who don't go they're nevertheless pleased it's there for bereavement, even if they believe nothing. It gives the required dignity to the end of someone's life.

Harry's asleep and tomorrow I know (well, think and hope) he'll wake up and make a cup of tea and life will go on. Supposing he conks out? Doesn't bear thinking about! Don't you dare conk out!!! Don't you dare die a lingering death either

– I don't want to live with misery!

The Canon said something interesting to me at breakfast when, for some reason, we were talking about funerals. He said he always tries to say words which will lighten the guilt which families always experience at the death of one of its members – especially of a husband or wife. Does death bring an awareness of guilt? All the things one should have been but wasn't? BUT!! There are always reasons why one wasn't what one should have been. The W.I. woman's confession shows me that.

CHAPTER

12

FLIGHT HOME AGAIN

The wake-up call came at three forty-five a.m. By four thirty we were on our way to the airport in the early morning light, driving south from Tiberias.

We passed a field of sunflowers, a peaceful sight of crowded yellow heads with dark brown centres, all of them turned towards the rising sun as though in greeting. They lit up the foreground with their cheerful colour. Behind them was a hazy outline of barren hills rising to an opaque sky.

Our road passed by Megiddo, where the end of the world would happen. Well, the end hadn't happened yet and really it was just a dread, or a threat – an imaginary ultimate finality. The human mind is unable to cope with eternity, nor with finality come to that.

A distant higher looming hazy outline had to be Mt. Carmel, another place I would have liked to have visited. It had been there that Elijah had challenged the four hundred and fifty prophets of Baal in order to prove to King Ahab that the one and only true God was the one he, Elijah, served.

Religion with its claims and counter claims was a total

mystery. There was nothing wrong with it, so far as I could make out, until people became over obsessed and were prepared to die for it – or kill for it. That was where it went wrong. 'Nothing in excess' had been inscribed in Apollo's temple at Delphi, which seemed to me eminently sensible as a warning against dogmatism or Godmatism.

We arrived at the Airport three hours before departure in order to have time enough for the many rigid security checks. The young Jewish American girl at a security counter wanted me (very inconveniently) to unlock, unstrap and open our largest suitcase. I wanted to hate her but she was charming and apologetic as she lifted out hastily packed garments. "We have to do this," she confessed as she examined with grave suspicion the ferrule to an umbrella at the bottom of the case. "It is for everyone's good we have to do these random checks," she went on. Her colleagues everywhere seemed to speak with American accents.

I really would have liked to spend time with them, to have asked them about their lives and what had brought them to Israel, but it was out of the question. I was a traveller, and they were doing their job protecting their fledgling country, newly hatched from the egg of it's-in-the-Bible beliefs. It was the cuckoo in the Palestinian nest, turfing out any unfortunates whose nest it really was.

"Do you have any gifts? Has anyone asked you to carry anything through for them?" The American girl unfolded various garments and laid them aside; she turned over a packet of gift cards wrapped in cellophane which I had bought from the orphanage.

The problem with well-mannered human beings is that they are so nice – so pleasant and impossible to dislike. But to get beneath the surface and dig out what is in their minds is to open that can of worms. It is better to keep to the outer packaging of a stranger, to admire the well groomed hair (or wig), to find pleasure in the features, and take at face value the smiling eyes.

I wanted to say to this American Jewess, 'Look! you've unpacked everything so *you* jolly well put it all back again! *You* struggle to close it! *You* fix the padlock and get that strap done up!'

When as a young man Elias Chacour had returned by boat to Haifa from his studies in Paris, he had been singled out because he was Palestinian. He'd been told to wait in a small room where he had then been subjected to a lengthy interrogation and told to strip. That had been the last straw and, defying the order, he had taken a book from his suitcase and announced calmly that he had absolutely no intention of stripping. Instead, he would sit and read until the customs officer agreed to let him go. To quote his own words: 'Our stalemate ended after eight nerve-wracking hours.' (Eight hours!) 'I did not strip, and was finally admitted to my home country. Outside the customs building my family swarmed around – concerned, relieved, thankful. From them I learned that travel anywhere, even by taxi, was frighteningly uncertain for all Palestinians. At any moment, you were subject to search and interrogation...'

I felt I'd like to return one day to live among the Palestinians, to experience what they had to endure. But I knew Harry would never agree to it. Usually, if I said I wanted to do something excruciatingly awful I could bring him round to doing something not so bad. But, as living with the Palestinians would be the ultimate of awfulness to him, such a tactic wasn't possible. I'd have nothing not so bad to fall back on. In truth, I was glad Harry wouldn't agree to it and would forbid me doing it alone. I was not so brave.

Meanwhile, there he was, smiling at the auburn-haired, brown-eyed American Jewess, and saying that 'Of course she had to do her duty, we quite understood and it was no trouble at all putting everything back, and not to give it another thought.' I tried not to glower at him – or her – as I jumbled everything up, then hissed: "There! You try to shut it now!"

"How do I shut it?"

"How does any suitcase shut!" I countered. "You have to heave the top to the bottom and pull the bloody zip – IF you can."

I left him to his new-found love who smiled her beautiful apologetic smile before moving on to her next victim. I went across to the Irish girl who was pink in the face and looking agitated. The contents of her hold-all were all over the counter. The young woman examining her luggage said: "Is this your candy? Did anybody give you anything to take home with you?"

"Why would anybody do that?"

"We are obliged to ask these questions."

"If I married an Israeli would I then lose my Irish citizenship?" she enquired.

The question was ignored. "What's in this tin box?"

"Sweeties." The usual two-second look was scarcely half a second.

"Can you open it, please?"

"Why should I open it? It's a present for my little sister."

A male colleague was called over, and the Irish girl repeated: "It's only sweeties," and her eyes sparkled flirtatiously at him.

I returned to Harry who by now had struggled sufficiently to get the first quarter of the zip done up. He was in a bad temper because I hadn't helped him. Together we managed to bring the two zippings together and get it closed, padlocked and strapped. Double security pass tags were stuck to the suitcase before it disappeared along the conveyor belt.

The Irish girl joined us in the departure lounge looking well pleased with herself. "He was gorgeous," she said. "I offered him a sweetie from the tin but he wouldn't take it. I think he fancied me."

I could overhear the W.I. woman at a table behind me, her committee-meeting voice rising above the lower key voices of her companions: "No, they left me alone! S'pose I've got an honest face! – Oh, ha, ha! No harm done if you smile at these people – Yes, let's face it, they have to be admired! After their suffering at the hands of Nazi Germany, not to mention all the other persecutions over the centuries, to have a homeland of their own now! – Yes, I grant you that, and they've jolly well worked for it! Driving along in the coach you could see what was Israeli and what was Arab – That's very true, but what are they doing about it? When I run out of money I get meself a job. It's their own silly fault! – Yes, when we get home just give me a few days to draw breath, and then we'll have a get together to sort out our photographs. – How many? Well, at a guess, I must have taken five hundred at the very least! – Yes, ain't it just!"

On the flight home I took out my note-book and scribbled my final impressions: *Don't know what to think about anything. Know what I ought to think but don't think – all very difficult.*

If God really exists, then why did he take so many

thousands of years before making himself known to men? And why first pick on a wandering nomad in the middle of some desert (Moab? Ur?? can't remember). Really, it's all most, MOST peculiar that very civilized and educated people go down on their knees and worship the Almighty who picked on this nomad called Abraham and told him to do all sorts of breaking-of-God's-own-commandment things, i.e. murder his son, Isaac, (same thing as sacrifice) and his other son, Ishmael, down in Mecca, born as a result of adultery. Well, that's how it all began, or so the Jews, Christians and Moslems claim.

God then promised the seeds of Abraham to multiply as the stars of heaven – and how! Israel's just full of Abraham's descendants homing in from all parts of the world. Why? Because certain people wanted to prove the Bible right – the ingathering of the Jews and all that, before the final something or another like the end of the world, the coming of the Messiah etc.

The ten tribes of the Northern Kingdom who got scattered and dispersed amongst the other nations and lost their Jewish identity seem to me eminently sensible. Presumably, if all twelve tribes had disappeared then there'd have been just a few ancient scrolls for people to mull over and be curious about. They would be as interested in Yahweh as archaeologists or anthropologists are about ancient pagan gods – Tammuz or Baal or Astarte.

There'd be no not-to-be-questioned scripture, no Bible, no Koran, because all would have petered out all those centuries B.C.

Maybe the really strange thing is that it hasn't petered out!!!??? Maybe it's all there staring me in the face and I'm just being cussed? Maybe God is just smiling, waiting for me to capitulate? A major disaster (or a little one) and I'm calling on him, bleating, 'Please God!' Pathetic! as Richard Dawkins would say. Or is God an innate part of every human being –

that spark of the divine? But the Bible! The trouble it's caused!

Harry nudged me and indicated the El Al stewardess who was passing with a trolley of drinks. He wanted red wine and we were handed transparent disposable mugs and a small bottle each. The stewardess was yet another beautiful young Jewess. There was not an Arab or a Palestinian Christian in sight, not a Moslem to be seen. Just Jews and European Christians. All these identifications because of the Bible – and, I supposed, only because of it.

"We really ought to throw the Bible out of the window and all begin again," I said to Harry. I hoped I'd said it quietly enough not to be overheard by the Canon and his wife seated in front of us.

Harry told me to stop being ridiculous. He then settled back for a long overdue snooze, whilst I thought about where I could possibly go next to find enlightenment.

GLOSSARY

ABRAHAM: The first Patriarch and founding father of the Jewish religion. Born in Ur (modern Iraq) he was divinely guided to Haran (Syria) and then to Canaan. When an old man he was told by God that his wife Sarah (also old) would miraculously conceive and give birth to a son Isaac. Testing Abraham's faith and obedience, God finally commanded him to sacrifice his beloved son. Abraham was obedient to God's command and had the knife raised to do the deed when God sent a ram to be sacrificed instead.

ADAM: The first man created by God. Although commanded not to eat from the tree of knowledge in the Garden of Eden, he was tempted by his wife, Eve, and they both ate it. Knowing they had done wrong, they tried to hide from God without success, and the whole world suffered the consequence of their disobedience which ended in death.

ADONIS: A beautiful youth beloved of Aphrodite, Greek goddess of love. He was killed by a wild boar while out hunting, causing great grief to Aphrodite.

AELIA CAPITOLINA: The name given by the Emperor Hadrian to his new city built c.130 A.D. on the site of Jerusalem after it had been destroyed by the Romans in 70 A.D.

AHAB: The eighth king of the Northern Kingdom of Israel (c.871-852 B.C.) He married Jezebel, a princess from Sidon, who worshipped pagan gods and persuaded Ahab to do the same. They defied the Prophet Elijah's warnings of God's anger, and both met violent deaths, said to be divine judgement.

AHURA MAZDA: The highest god in Zoroastrianism. Ahura means 'light' and Mazda means 'wisdom', making Ahura Mazda the god of light and wisdom.

AKIVA, Rabbi: Second century A.D. He was a strong supporter of Simeon Bar Kokhba, leader of the second Jewish revolt (132-135A.D.), regarding him as the long awaited Messiah.

ALEXANDER THE GREAT: (356-323 B.C.) King of Macedon, a state in northern Greece. He was tutored by Aristotle, and his military genius won him a vast empire stretching from the Adriatic in the west as far east as India. His conquests spread Greek culture and beliefs.

al-KHADER: A Moslem word for St. George.

al-LLAH: The pagan pre-Moslem High God of Mecca.

ALLAH: The Arabic name for God. Islam regards Allah as being One, Invisible, Eternal, Indivisible, Beneficient, Almighty, All-knowing, Omnipresent, Just, Merciful, Loving and Forgiving.

al-LAT: One of the three daughters of al-Llah.

al-UZZAH: One of the three daughters of al-Llah.

AMAZIAH: King of Judah (796-782 B.C.)

ANDREW: One of the twelve disciples, brother of Peter.

ANTONY, Mark: (c.82-30 B.C.) A Roman politician and general known as Marcus Antonius. He was a loyal supporter of Julius Caesar who was his mother's cousin. He became renowned for his love of Cleopatra, queen of Egypt.

APHRODITE: Greek goddess of love.

APOLLO: God of music and prophecy, son of Zeus.

ARK OF THE COVENANT: A box-like container of wood overlaid with gold, containing the two tablets of the Decalogue (the ten commandments). It was kept in the Holy of Holies in the first temple at Jerusalem but was lost when the city fell to the Babylonians.

ARMAGEDDON: The final battle at the end of the world between the forces of good and evil, expected to take place at Megiddo.

ASCLEPIUS: God of medicine, and son of Apollo.

ASTARTE: The Semitic goddess of fertility, equated by the Greeks with Aphrodite.

ATHENA: Greek goddess of wisdom, arts and crafts. She was born fully armed from the head of Zeus, and was patron goddess of Athens.

ATONEMENT: Because of sin there is a separation of men from God, and their hope is to be made 'at one' with God again – hence the word 'atonement'.

AUGUSTUS: The title taken by Octavian, great nephew and adopted son of Julius Caesar who became emperor 27 B.C. -14 A.D.

BAAL: The fertility god of the Canaanites, believed to be in eternal conflict with Mot, god of death and infertility.

BACCHUS: Roman name for Dionysos, Greek god of wine and drama.

BALFOUR, Arthur James: (1848-1930) British foreign secretary 1916-1919.

BALFOUR DECLARATION: A letter dated 2nd November, 1917, written by Balfour to the wealthy and influential Jew, Lord Rothschild, declaring Britain's support for a Jewish homeland in Palestine. It was Balfour's Declaration which resulted in the League of Nations entrusting Britain with the Mandate of Palestine in 1922.

BAR KOKHBA: A Messianic title, meaning 'Son of a Star'. It was taken by Bar Koziba (see below).

BAR KOZIBA, Simeon: A second century A.D. rebel commander who led the Jewish revolt against the Romans from 132 A.D. till his death in 135 A.D. He used the title 'Bar Kokhba' and was regarded by some as the Messiah.

BAR MITZVAH: The Hebrew for 'son of commandment'. The ritual undertaken by a Jewish boy at the age of thirteen when he is considered to be old enough to be responsible for his religious observances.

BATTLE of BADR: The first major battle between Muhammad and his followers and the pagan Meccans in 623 A.D.

BATTLE of UHUD: A major battle in 625 A.D. between the Prophet and the Quraysh, Muhammad's original tribe at Mecca. Muhammad himself was wounded and his army routed.

BEATITUDES: The statements of blessing in Jesus' Sermon on the Mount (Matthew 5:3-12).

BEGIN, Menachem: (1913-1992) One of the pioneering Zionists in Palestine, whose terrorist activities caused the British to pull out in 1948 which resulted in The War of Independence and the founding of The State of Israel. He became Israel's Prime Minister in 1977.

BEN GURION, David: (1886-1973) Israeli statesman, and early pioneer. He moulded the new State of Israel after the War of Independence and the withdrawal of the British in 1948, and became Israel's first Prime Minister.

CALIPH: Title taken by Muhammad's immediate successors. Later there were many caliphs, and they were seen as representatives of God on earth.

CANAANITES: Descendants of Canaan, grandson of Noah.

CELSUS: Second century pagan philosopher. He wrote his *True Discourse,* a satirical attack on Christianity c.178, which has survived in Origen's *Contra Celsus.*

CHACOUR, Elias: A Palestinian Christian, and author of *Blood Brothers* and *We Belong to the Land.*

CHANUKKAH: An eight-day Jewish festival of lights usually held in mid-December. It celebrates the victory of the Maccabees in 165 B.C. over the Seleucid rulers of Palestine who had desecrated the Temple and imposed their Hellenistic religion.

CHRISTIAN ZIONISTS: They believe that the 'ingathering' of the Jews to the 'promised land', will hurry on the Second Coming of Jesus.

CHURCH FATHERS: Early influential Christian theologians and teachers.

CLEOPATRA: (68-30 B.C.) Queen of Egypt.

CONSTANTINE THE GREAT: (274-337 A.D.) Roman emperor. He was the first emperor to accept Christianity as a true religion, though he continued to honour the old Roman gods.

CYRIL, St.: (c.315-386 A.D.) Bishop of Jerusalem from c.349.

DAVID, King: First king of the United Kingdom of Israel and Judah. He was the youngest son of Jesse, a farmer in Bethlehem, and looked after his father's flocks. God sent the prophet Samuel to anoint him king.

DAYAN, Moshe: (1915-1981) Israeli military leader and politician with enormous charisma, dash and daring, who became famous for his eye-patch after he lost an eye when a Vichy French rifle bullet shattered his binoculars in the second world war. He was born of Ukrainian parents in Kibbutz Deganiah and, at the age of fourteen joined the Haganah, the Jewish underground self-defence organization. He went on to become Chief of Staff of the Israeli Defence Forces, and Minister of Defence.

DEAD SEA SCROLLS: A collection of 972 manuscripts discovered in caves twenty miles east of Jerusalem between 1947 and 1956.

DEMETER: Greek goddess of corn.

DEMETRIUS, St.: Appointed bishop of Alexandria in 189 A.D.

DESCARTES, René: (1596-1650) French philosopher.

DIONYSOS: Greek god of wine and drama.

DIONYSIUS: After hearing St. Paul preach he converted to Christianity. He is commonly known as Dionysius the Areopagite because St. Paul addressed the Athenians from an elevation known as the Areopagus in Athens.

DOME OF THE ROCK: A golden dome rising from an octagonal base under which is the Rock on which Abraham prepared to sacrifice his son Isaac. It is believed to have been the Holy of Holies in Solomon's temple. The Dome of the Rock was built in 691 A.D.

EID al-FITR: The breaking of the Ramadan fast which begins at the sighting of the new moon at the end of the month of Ramadan. The festival lasts three days.

ELIJAH: Ninth century B.C. prophet of the Northern Kingdom of Israel, who protested about King Ahab's worship of pagan gods. He is expected to return before the final Day of Judgement and the coming of the Messiah.

ESSENES: A Jewish sect which flourished from the second century B.C. to the destruction of the temple in 70 A.D. It is generally believed that the Dead Sea Scrolls came from the Essenes at Qumran.

ESTHER: A Jewess, usually dated to the third or fourth century B.C. She hid her Jewish identity from her husband the Persian king. When she learned that the king's chief minister planned to annihilate all the Jews in the kingdom, she pleaded with her husband and, with the help of God, the Jews survived. It was regarded as another deliverance and is celebrated annually at the Jewish feast of Purim.

EURIPIDES: (c.480-406 B.C.) Greek writer of tragedies.

EUSEBIUS: (265-340 A.D.) Bishop of Caesarea, and author of *Ecclesiastical History.*

EVE: The first woman created by God to be a companion to Adam. She was tempted by the serpent in the Garden of Eden, and ate of the fruit of the Tree of Knowledge, so bringing death into the world.

EZEKIEL: A prophet at the time of the Babylonian exile, who called his people to repentance.

FESTIVAL OF LIGHTS: (see CHANUKKAH).

GABRIEL, The angel: One of seven archangels, who was sent by God to Zechariah to announce the future birth of a son, John the Baptist. He was sent also to the Virgin Mary to announce her immaculate conception and the birth of Jesus.

GENTILES: Non-Jews.

GEORGE, St.: Martyr of the third or fourth century, and patron saint of soldiers. He is generally believed to have been from Cappadocia. After performing many miracles, he was tortured and beheaded by the Emperor Diocletian. The myth of him killing a dragon was a late medieval addition. His feast day is 23rd April.

GNOSTICISM: A religious movement which emerged strongly in the second century A.D., the central idea being that 'gnosis' (revealed knowledge of God) was brought by Christ from the supreme God who was the unknowable Divine Being of which all humans had a spark. The God of the Old Testament, they claimed, was a Demiurge who had been the creator of this imperfect world, and Christ had come as an emissary sent by the Divine Being to bring 'gnosis' (knowledge). Jesus, they asserted, had not been in any way mortal, and had not died, he had merely appeared as a phantom, assuming human appearance only.

GOLDSTEIN, Baruch: (1956-1994). An American-born Jewish fanatic who, during the Jewish feast of Purim, carried out a mass murder of Moslem worshippers at the Cave of the Patriarchs at Hebron in 1994 (see PURIM). He killed 29 Palestinians and wounded 125. He was regarded by many Jewish extremists as a national hero and saint.

GOSPELS, The: Four Gospels of the New Testament: Matthew, Mark, Luke and John. There are many heretical gospels, known as the Apocryphal, which are of a later date.

HADES: The Greek god of the underworld.

HADRIAN: Roman emperor (117-138 A.D.)

HAGANAH: A secret Jewish paramilitary organization set up in Palestine in defiance of the British Mandate which declared it illegal for Jews to carry arms.

HANINA, ben Dosa: A pious miracle worker of the first century A.D. who lived in Galilee.

HARAM al-SHARIF: Site of the Dome of the Rock and the al-Aqsa mosque. Known to the Jews as the Temple Mount.

HAREDIM: Ultra-Orthodox religious Jews who believe they belong to a chain going back to Moses.

HELENA, St.: Mother of Constantine the Great.

HELLENISTS: A term applied to the Greek civilization following the death of Alexander the Great.

HERA: Greek goddess of marriage, wife and sister of Zeus.

HEROD THE GREAT: He was made procurator of Judaea by Julius Caesar in 47 B.C. The Romans gave him the title of 'king of the Jews' and he reigned as king from 37-4 B.C. He was hated by the Jews although he spent a lot of money on the temple and other building projects.

HEROD ANTIPAS: Son of Herod the Great. He ruled Galilee 4 B.C.-39A.D. He imprisoned John the Baptist and it was he who had him beheaded at his wife's request. It was to Herod Antipas that Pilate handed Jesus over for trial because he came from Galilee.

HERZL, Theodor: (1860-1904) An Austrian-Hungarian Jew, and father of modern Zionism and consequently the State of Israel.

HEZEKIAH: King of Judah 716-687 B.C.

HOMER: The great epic poet of ancient Greece, author of *The Iliad* and *The Odyssey*. He is believed to have lived in the seventh or eighth century B.C.

IRGUN: An offshoot of Haganah (see above). It was a paramilitary Zionist group which operated in Palestine between 1931 and 1948.

ISAAC: Son of Abraham and Sarah, born to them in their old age.

ISAIAH: An eighth century B.C. prophet who lived in Jerusalem.

JACOB: Abraham's grandson, son of Isaac and Rebecca.

JAMES: The brother of Jesus. He became the leader of the Church in Jerusalem, and is believed to have been stoned to death in 62 A.D.

JEREMIAH: Prophet of Judah who lived in the seventh century B.C.

JEROME, St.: (c.342-420 A.D.) His greatest achievement was the translation of most of the Bible into Latin, which became known as the Vulgate.

JESSE: Father of King David.

JEZEBEL: Wife of King Ahab of Israel who worshipped idols and persuaded her husband to do the same. She killed the prophets of God and replaced them with the prophets of Baal, but Elijah escaped and Jezebel met a violent end, as did Ahab also —said to be God's judgement.

JOACHIM: The father of the Virgin Mary.

JOHN THE BAPTIST: Son of Zachariah and Elizabeth, and born to them in old age. His birth was foretold by the angel Gabriel, who said that he would have 'the power and spirit of Elijah' on him. It was John who baptized his followers in the river Jordan and told them that one mightier than he was to come.

JOSEPH: Husband of the Virgin Mary, and the legal father of Jesus, though not his actual father as Mary had immaculately conceived.

JOSEPHUS, Flavius: (c.37-c.100 A.D.) Jewish historian made famous by *The Jewish War* and *Antiquities of the Jews.*

JOSHUA: He took over the leadership of the Israelites after the death of Moses, and led them to the 'promised land'. His name in Hebrew means 'God is my salvation'.

JULIAN THE APOSTATE: (332-363 A.D.) Roman emperor from 361 who tried to turn people back to the pagan gods. He was a nephew of Constantine and, although brought up a Christian, preferred the old gods.

JUSTINIAN: (483-565 A.D.) Roman emperor from 527A.D. A confirmed Christian who built many churches and closed down the philosophical schools in Athens.

KA'BAH: The large cubic-stone structure at the heart of Mecca. It is covered in a black cloth (the *kiswah*) woven in gold thread with inscriptions from the Koran, and is the central point of worship for Moslems.

KHADIJAH: The first wife of Muhammad.

KNESSET: The Israeli parliament.

KOOK, Rabbi Abraham Isaac: (1865-1935) Chief Rabbi of the Holy Land. He believed the world was progressing to a new consciousness, and the return of the Jewish People to their ancestral home was a sign of the Messianic redemption.

KORAN: The holy book of Islam.

KOCHBA, Simeon Bar: (See Bar Kochba).

LAZARUS: Friend of Jesus and brother of Martha and Mary. Jesus raised Lazarus from the dead.

LEAH: Wife of Jacob, the third patriarch.

MACCABEES: The celebrated Jewish family who led the revolt against the Seleucid rulers of Palestine in 168 B.C.

MAGDALENE, Mary: Generally believed to have been a prostitute. She became a close companion of Jesus after he cast out seven demons from her, and was present at Christ's crucifixion. She was also the first to find his empty tomb and to see the risen Christ.

MAGI: The first non-Jews to believe in Christ. They were probably astrologers, maybe of the Zoroastrian religion in Persia. It was the Church Father, Origen, who first said there were three.

MAIMONIDES, Moses: (1136-1204 A.D.) A renowned Jewish philospher who wrote a treatise *Guide for the Perplexed* in which he tried to reconcile human reason as argued by Aristotle with Jewish revelation. Born in Spain his family fled to Egypt where he became physician to Saladin.

MANAT: One of the three daughters of al-Llah at Mecca.

MARTHA: Sister of Mary and Lazarus.

MARY: Sister of Martha and Lazarus.

MARY: The Virgin Mary, mother of Jesus.

MEIR, Golda: (1898-1978). The fourth prime minister of Israel. Born in Kiev, she was regarded as the personification of the Zionist spirit.

MENORAH: The seven-branched gold candelabrum, the original of which was kept burning at all times in the Jerusalem Temple. Today it is the emblem of the State of Israel.

MERCURIUS, St.: A soldier saint who fought under the Emperor Decius against invading barbarians. Legend has it that the Archangel Michael appeared to him holding a shining sword and told him to take it to help defeat these enemies of God. He was executed when he refused to join in the emperor's pagan sacrifice. It was later said that it was the martyred St. Mercurius who killed Julian the Apostate in Persia 363 A.D.

MESSIAH: From the Hebrew 'mashiah', meaning 'anointed'. He is expected by the Jews to be the anointed king of the House of David, to be sent by God to bring about the final redemption in the End of Days.

MIKVEH: Water from rain or from a spring used for ritual purification of Jews.

MOSES: Chosen by God to lead the Israelites out of Egypt. He received the tablets of the decalogue (the ten commandments) and the oral Torah while up Mount Sinai.

NEBUCHADNEZZAR: King of Babylon (605-562 B.C.) When the king of Judah rebelled against Babylonian tax, Nebuchadnezzar destroyed Jerusalem and took the Judaean leaders into exile to Babylon.

NEOPLATONISM: The philosophical system of Plotinus (c.205-270 A.D.) They tried to prove by intellectual argument the basis for a religious and moral life.

ORIGEN: (c.185-254 A.D.) Theologian and biblical critic. He became bishop of Alexandria and ended up in Caesarea where he founded a school of theology.

PAN: Greek god of flocks and shepherds. Originally an Arcadian deity. He invented the musical pipe of seven reeds, known as the Pan pipes.

PASSOVER: See Pesach.

PAUL, St.: Born in Tarsus and originally called Saul, he was a Jew with Roman citizenhip. He was at first fiercely opposed to the Christians till a vision on the road to Damascus turned him as fiercely Christian. After his conversion he went about preaching and converting the gentiles. He is believed to have been martyred at Rome under the Emperor Nero between 62-64 A.D.

PENTECOST: The equivalent of the Jewish Shavuot festival. It falls on the fiftieth day after Passover. The disciples (who were Jews) were celebrating Shavuot in the Upper Room when the Holy Spirit descended on them in tongues of fire.

PESACH: The Jewish Passover feast celebrated annually to commemorate the Israelite deliverance from Egypt under Moses.

PETER: Chief of the disciples of Jesus and brother of Andrew. He and Andrew were fishermen. After seeing the risen Christ following the crucifixion, he turned his whole attention to the spreading of the Gospel.

PHOEBOS APOLLO: An epithet for the Greek god Apollo, meaning 'Apollo the shining one'.

PILATE, Pontius: The Roman governor (procurator) of Judaea 26-36 A.D. When Jesus was brought before him to be tried, he feared a riot and being removed from office as a consequence, so washed his hands of the matter thus allowing the crucifixion to take place.

PLATO: (c.427-347 B.C.) Greek philosopher, and pupil of Socrates.

PURIM: A minor Jewish festival celebrating the story of the Book of Esther (see Esther).

RABIN, Yitzhak: (1922-1995) Israeli politician, statesman and general. He was the fifth Prime Minister of Israel from 1974-1977, and again in 1992 until his assassination. He met his death at the hands of a radical right-wing Orthodox Jew who objected to his role in the signing of the Oslo Accords which gave the Palestinians more power over certain parts of the Gaza Strip and the West Bank.

RAMADAN: A month of fasting for Moslems beginning at the first sighting of the new moon. Fasting begins from the first thread of light seen on the horizon till the sun has set. The feast of Eid al-Fitr, marks the breaking of the Ramadan fast.

REBECCA: Wife of Isaac.

SALADIN: Salah ad-Din, Yusuf ibn Ayyub. (1137/8-1193). A Kurdish military leader who became sultan of an extensive empire. He was generous minded and, although he won back Jerusalem from Richard Coeur de Lyon in the Third Crusade, he treated him with respect and as a friend.

SAMARITANS: Descendants of the Israelites of the Northern Kingdom of Israel whose capital was Samaria.

SARAH: Abraham's wife, and mother of Isaac.

SATAN: The personification of all that is evil and opposed to God.

SCAPEGOAT: At the festival of Yom Kippur two goats would be selected. One would be chosen by lot to be sacrificed to God, and the other (the scapegoat) had the sins of the people of Israel recited over it before it was sent out into the wilderness to certain death.

SELEUCIDS: After the death of Alexander the Great his empire in the Middle East was divided between two of his generals one of whom was Seleucus who ruled Syria.

SHAVUOT: Hebrew for Pentecost (see Pentecost).

SHOFAR: The Hebrew for 'horn'. An ancient instrument used to summon the people to repentance. The most commonly used is a hollowed out ram's horn.

SOCRATES: (469-399 B.C.) An Athenian philosopher. He was found guilty and sentenced to death for allegedly corrupting the minds of the young by introducing strange gods. He accepted the verdict and approached death with philosophical interest before drinking the hemlock.

SOL INVICTUS: The invincible sun. The official sun god of the later Roman Empire. The Emperor Aurelian in the third century A.D. made it an official cult along with the other Roman cults. The celebration of the birth of Sol Invictus was 25th December.

SOLOMON: The third king of Israel from 970 B.C. Son of King David and Bathsheba. He died c.930 B.C.

SOPHRONIUS, St.: (c.560-638 A.D.) Patriarch of Jerusalem from 634 A.D.

STERN GANG: Zionist extremist organisation in Palestine, founded in 1940 by Avraham Stern, as an anti-British terrorist group.

TALMUD: Hebrew for 'study'. The most important work of the oral Torah (see Torah).

TAMMUZ: A very early Babylonian and Assyrian god, equated by the Greeks with Adonis. His spouse was Ishtar, the Babylonian fertility goddess, sometimes known as Ashtart, or Astarte, later equated by the Greeks with Aphrodite.

TEMPLE MOUNT: The Jewish name for Haram al-Sharif (Arabic for the Noble Sanctuary). It is the holiest site in Jerusalem as it is the site of the rock where Abraham prepared to sacrifice his son Isaac.

TORAH: The Hebrew for 'teaching'. It generally refers to the Jewish teaching of the Pentateuch, and in its widest sense to the whole of the Jewish tradition.

UMAR, Caliph: The second Caliph, one of the four Patriarchal Caliphs of the seventh century A.D.

VENUS: Roman goddess of love.

VIRGIN MARY: The mother of Jesus. When she was betrothed to Joseph the angel Gabriel told her she had immaculately conceived. Her perpetual virginity was first insisted upon in the fifth century.

WAILING WALL: Otherwise known as the Western Wall, the only remaining structure of Herod's Second Temple destroyed by the Romans in 70 A.D. It is today a site of Jewish pilgrimage and prayer.

YAHWEH: The Hebrew name for God.

YOM KIPPUR: The Hebrew for 'Day of Atonement'. The most sacred day of the Jewish year which ends ten days of penitence.

YOM KIPPUR WAR: Otherwise known as the October War. It was fought by Israel from 6th-25th October, 1973, against the Arab coalition forces led by Egypt and Syria. The latter chose the Jewish holy day of Yom Kippur for attacking Israel knowing that the Israeli military would be celebrating with their families. The Israelis, however, counter-attacked with surprising ferocity and drove back the enemy.

ZACHARIAH: Priest, and father of John the Baptist.

ZARATHUSTRA: Also known as Zoroaster. A religious leader who, around 600 B.C., brought the Persian people back to their ancient Zoroastrian religion, and wrote the *Zend-Avesta,* the bible of this religion.

ZEALOTS: A group of nationalists who kept alive the Maccabean spirit of guerilla warfare against Roman rule.

ZECHARIAH: Minor Old Testament prophet of the sixth century B.C. He predicted the rebuilding of the Jerusalem temple under a new ruler of the Davidic line.

ZEUS: Supreme Olympian Greek god. He was god of the sky and the weather, and in classical times became protector of law and justice.

BIBLIOGRAPHY

Abu El-Assal, Riah, *Caught in Between,* SPCK, 1999.

Allegro, J.M., *The Dead Sea Scrolls.* Penguin Books, 1956.

Andrae, Tor, *Mohammed: The Man and His Faith.* The Dover edition, 2000.

Andrews, Richard, *Blood on the Mountain, A History of the Temple Mount from the Ark of the Covenant to the Third Millennium.* Phoenix, 2000.

Armstrong, Karen, *Muhammad. A Biography of the Prophet.* Phoenix Press, 2001.

Armstrong, Karen, *A History of Jerusalem, One City, Three Faiths.* Harper Perennial, London 1996.

Baigent, Michael, and Richard Leigh, *The Dead Sea Scrolls Deception.* Arrow Books, 2001.

Ben-Gurion, *Ben-Gurion looks back in talks with Moshe Pearlman.* Weidenfeld and Nicolson, 1965.

Bowen, Jeremy, *Six Days, How the 1967 War Shaped the Middle East.* Simon and Schuster, 2003.

Carter, Jimmy, *Palestine, Peace not Apartheid.* Simon & Schuster UK Ltd., 2006.

Chacour, Elias, *Blood Brothers.* Chosen Books, 1984.

Chacour, Elias, *We Belong to the Land.* University of Notre Dame, Indiana, 2001.

Chapman, Colin, *Whose Promised Land?* A Lion Hudson plc, 1983.

Cline, Eric H., *Jerusalem Besieged, From Ancient Canaan to Modern Israel.* University of Michigan Press, 2004.

Curzon, The Honourable Robert, *Visits to Monasteries in the Levant.* Arthut Baker Ltd., London, 1995.

Dayan, Moshe, *Story of My Life.* Weidenfeld and Nicolson Ltd., 1976.

Dosick, Rabbi Wayne, *Living Judaism, the complete guide to Jewish belief, tradition, and practice.* Harper, San Fransisco, 1995.

Eusebius, *The History of the Church from Christ to Constantine,* translated by G.A. Williamson, Penguin Books, 1965.

Eusebius, *Life of Constantine,* translated with introduction and commentary by Averil Cameron and Stuart G. Hall, O.U.P., 1999.

Flusser, David, *The Spiritual History of the Dead Sea Sect.* MOD Books, 1989.

Gilbert, Martin, *Israel, A History.* Black Swan, 1998.

Glass, Cyril, *The New Encyclopedia of Islam.* AltaMira Press, 1989.

Goldberg, David J., and Rayner, John D., *The Jewish People. Their History and Their Religion.* Penguin Books, 1987.

Gospel of Judas, edited by Rodolphe Kasser, Marvin Meyer, and Gregor Wurst. Published by the National Geographic Society, 2006.

Guardia, Anton la, *Holy Land Unholy War, Israelis and Palestinians.* John Murray, 2001.

Hart, Alan, *Arafat (Terrorist or Peacemaker?)* Sidgwick & Jackson, London, 1984.

Hirst, David, *The Gun and the Olive Branch.* Faber and Faber, 1977.

Hroub, Khaled, *Hamas, A Beginner's Guide.* Pluto Press, 2006.

Israeli, Raphael, *Green Crescent Over Nazareth.* Frank Cass Publishers, 2002.

Josephus, Flavius, *The Jewish War.* Penguin Books, 1959.

Josephus, Flavius, *Antiquities of the Jews.* T. Nelson and Sons, 1883.

The Koran, with a Parallel Arabic Text, translated with notes by N.J. Dawood. Penguin Books.

Kriwaczek, Paul, *In Search of Zarathustra.* Phoenix paperback, 2002.

Lane Fox, Robin, *Alexander the Great.* Penguin Books, 1973.

McDowall, David, *The Palestinians, The Road to Nationhood.* Minority Rights Group, 1994.

Makiya, Kanan, *The Rock, A Tale of Seventh-century Jerusalem.* Constable, 2001.

Masalha, Nur, *The Bible and Zionism.* Zed Books, 2007.

Origen *Contra Celsus,* translated by Henry Chadwick. Cambridge University Press, 1953.

Pearlman, Moshe, *The Zealots of Masada.* Palphot Ltd., 1966.

Schauss, Hayyim, *The Jewish Festivals, A guide to their history and observance.* Schocken Books, 1962.

Shahak, Israel and Mezvinsky, Norton, *Jewish Fundamentalism in Israel.* Pluto Press, 2004.

Sizer, Stephen, *Christian Zionism.* Inter-Varsity Press, 2004.

St. John, Robert, *Ben-Gurion.* Jarrolds Publishers. London 1959.

Unterman, Alan, *Dictionary of Jewish Lore and Legend.* Thames and Hudson, 1991.

Worth, Richard, *Ariel Sharon.* Chelsea House Publishers, 2003.

Jill Dudley was born in Baghdad and educated in England. She had her first play performed by the Leatherhead Repertory Company and, since then, has written plays and short stories for Radio.

She returned to Iraq in 1956 when her husband was working out there and, after the Iraqi revolution, came back to England where she and her husband bought a dairy farm. When they retired from farming in 1990 they began to travel.

Her travel books *Ye Gods! (travels in Greece), Ye Gods! II (more travels in Greece), and Holy Smoke! (travels in Turkey and Egypt)* are the result of their earlier journeys.